Animal Tracks

Todd Telander

FALCONGUIDES

GUILFORD, CONNECTICUT
HELENA, MONTANA

AN IMPRINT OF GLOBE PEQUOT PRESS

To my wife, Kirsten, my children, Miles and Oliver, and my parents, all of whom have supported and encouraged me through the years. Special thanks to Jim Halfpenny for his expert and gracious assistance in developing the illustrations, and for sharing his vast knowledge of tracking.

To buy books in quantity for corporate use or incentives, call **(800) 962-0973** or e-mail **premiums@GlobePequot.com**.

FALCONGUIDES®

Illustrations by Todd Telander
Text design: Sheryl P. Kober
Project editor: David Legere
Layout: Sue Murray

Library of Congress Cataloging-in-Publication Data is available on file.

ISBN 978-0-7627-7415-9

Printed in the United States of America

10 9 8 7 6 5 4 3 2 1

Contents

Mammals

Birds

Reptiles

Amphibians

Introduction

The tracks that animals leave are not only indications of what species they are but also clues as to their life history, habitats, and movements. Wild animals are generally wary of humans, and much of their activity remains undetected by our eyes. But even if they themselves are not seen, they leave a record of their existence by their tracks. This book is designed to serve as an introduction to recognizing and appreciating the hundreds of different kinds of tracks that we can find in the United States, and includes those of mammals, birds, reptiles, and amphibians. With keen observence, not only will you be better able to determine which animal made a certain track, but you will also allow yourself to become closer to their world, their habits, and their secrets. I list here some of the more common animal tracks you are likely to encounter in the United States. There are, of course, many others that are not included, but most will be similar to the individual species or animal families listed here, and will give you a starting point to refining your searches and your understanding of the wild world, from mountaintops to seashores to desert plains.

Notes about the Species Accounts

Names

The common name as well as the scientific name is included for each entry. Since common names tend to vary regionally, or there may be more than one common name for each species, the universally accepted scientific name of genus and species (such as *Spermophilus lateralis* for the golden-mantled ground squirrel) is more reliable to be certain of identification. Also, one can often learn interesting facts about an animal by the English translation of its Latin name. For instance, the generic name, *Spermophilus,* means "lover of seeds," and the specific name, *lateralis,* relates to the lateral striping on the sides of the squirrel.

Families

Animals are grouped into families based on similar traits, behaviors, and genetics. I include the family names for each animal to clarify its relationship to other species in the same family, and to hopefully make it easier to identify an unfamiliar track. For example, members of the mustelid family all have five toes on the front and rear feet, with a small and less pronounced inner toe. So if you see this pattern, it makes sense to look in the section on mustelids and narrow your search from there.

Size/Weight

The size given for each animal is the average length, and for some animals the tail length is given separately. Weight is also an average. Keep in mind that many animals exhibit tremendous variability in size and weight, and that males and females may differ in size.

Range

Range is the general geographic space that a species occupies, and in this book includes only those areas within the United States. Range and habitat must be considered together to determine if a given animal is likely to be found in a given area.

Habitat

Habitat includes the local conditions of climate, vegetation, soil types, water availability, elevation, and terrain. Some animals have very specific habitat requirements, while others may occupy just about any habitat within their range.

Track Size

The size of tracks is given as an average measurement of width by length. Separate measurements are given for front and rear feet, except for the birds (who only have one set of legs). If parts of the track are usually evident and diagnostic, like claws and heel pads, then they are included in the measurement. If not, they are omitted from the measurement and mentioned in the text. In the field, the size of a track can vary quite a bit depending on the substrate or how the animal was moving. Toes may also spread in loose soils or snow, which can increase the width of the track considerably.

Illustrations

The illustrations show the right side front and rear feet of each animal. For birds, the left and right foot are shown. I have illustrated the tracks to show the basic pattern and all components of the footprint that may register. It is important to remember that a perfect track is rare—most are quite vague, messy, and lack many of the features that are written about or illustrated. Use the illustrations to help visualize the fundamental pattern and organization of the foot, not necessarily as template for a perfect match.

Track Topography and Terms

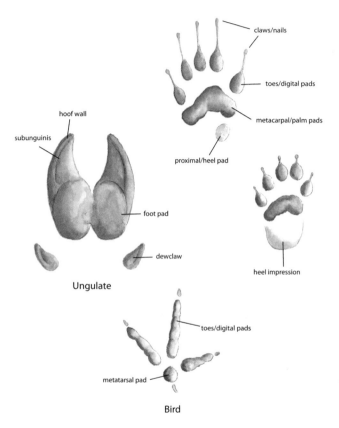

claws/nails

toes/digital pads

metacarpal/palm pads

hoof wall

subunguinis

proximal/heel pad

foot pad

dewclaw

heel impression

Ungulate

toes/digital pads

metatarsal pad

Bird

MAMMALS

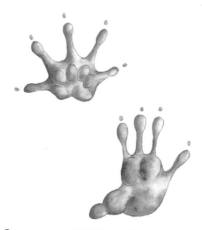

Virginia Opossum, *Didelphis virginiana*
Family Didelphidae (Skunks)
Size/Weight: approx. 30" long with tail; approx. 10 lbs.
Range: Central and eastern United States, portions of Pacific states
Habitat: Woodlands, riparian zones, urban areas, farms
The Virginia opossum is a marsupial, meaning it bears premature young to develop in an external pouch, and is the only member of this group in North America. It is stocky, with relatively small limbs, a pointed snout, and a long, round, hairless tail. The color is mottled grayish with a white face and dark ears. It is nocturnal, mostly solitary, and reasonably adept at swimming and climbing. It has a highly varied diet that includes nuts, fruit, insects, small animals, and carrion. Opossums have a curious habit of feigning death when under attack, then resuming as normal once safe.

Track size (front): 2" wide x 1¾" long
Track size (rear): 2" wide x 2" long
Description of Track: The front foot is noticeably wider than the rear. There are five toes on both the front and rear feet. The rear foot has an unusual "opposable" thumb as the inner digit, is unclawed, and appears quite separate from the other toes. The claws may or may not register in the track. There are six, fairly distinct metacarpal and proximal pads on the front, while those on the rear are larger and less obvious. Tail drag may obscure the track in a walk, but the tail is held upright in faster gaits.

Shrew, *Sorex* spp. and others

Family Sorcidae (Shrews)

Size/Weight: approx. 3–5" long with tail; approx. ¼ oz.

Range: Throughout the United States

Habitat: Extremely varied; forests, open fields, marshes

Shrews are our smallest mammals and are unrelated to the rodents. They are very active and shaped like elongate mice with sharply pointed heads, tiny eyes, and long, lightly furred tails. Their fine, dense fur ranges from gray, brown, to black with a paler underside.

Track size (front): ¼" wide x ¼" long

Track size (rear): ¼" wide x ⅓" long

Description of Track: There are five toes on both front and rear feet, unlike rodents that show only four toes on the front foot. Claws are substantial and usually show in the track. The metacarpal pads are fairly distinct, showing a group of three on the front foot, with three proximal pads below, and on the rear foot there are four metacarpal pads and two proximal pads. These are the smallest mammal tracks you will find in the United States.

Pika, *Ochotona princeps*
Family Ochotonidae (Pikas)
Size/Weight: approx. 8" long; approx. 5 oz.
Range: Western US mountains
Habitat: High-altitude rocky slopes

The pika is a small, plump animal of the mountains that is related to the rabbits. It has a relatively large head, rounded ears, and a tiny tail that is usually not visible in the field. Its fur is thick and colored pale grayish brown. It is often detected by its high-pitched, squeaking call, and makes tunnels through the snow in winter that leave traces on the ground upon snowmelt. Active during the day, mostly solitary and moving about in slow bounds, pikas forage on grasses and herbs, which they store in large piles like hay for lean winter months.

Track size (front): ¾" wide x ¾" long
Track size (rear): ¾" wide x 1" long
Description of Track: The front foot has five toes with the inner toe being smaller and not always registering, and the rear foot has four toes. The small claws may or may not register. Toe pads are clearer than those of rabbits, but the rest of the foot is heavily furred and leaves an indistinct impression. The hind track may be rounded or show some heel.

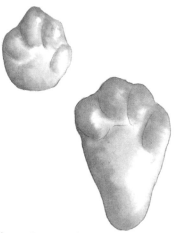

Snowshoe Hare, *Lepus americanus*

Family Leporidae (Rabbits, Hares)
Size/Weight: approx. 15" long; approx. 3 lbs.
Range: Northern and mountainous United States
Habitat: Forests, mountains, swamps

The snowshoe hare is an animal of the north, with long ears, a short, round tail, and especially large rear feet that give traction in snow. During the summer, it is grayish brown with a pale under-side, while in the winter it changes to snow-white except for its large, dark eyes and black-tipped ears. The color change aids in camouflage as the snows of winter arrive. It is primarily noctur-nal and solitary, and feeds on herbs and grasses in summer, and branches and bark in winter, but will also eat meat if available.

Track size (front): 1¾" wide x 2" long
Track size (rear): 4" wide x 5" long
Description of Track: The rear foot is noticeably larger than the front. There are five toes on the front foot, but only four reliably register. The rear foot has four toes. The claws are short and not evident. Toe pads, metacarpal pads, and heel are reduced and concealed by heavy fur, so the track is indistinct. The front track is rounded, while the rear is long, often pointed, and can splay widely. The trail pattern of the hop shows the front feet one in front of the other, seldom side by side as in squirrels.

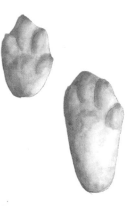

Cottontail Rabbit, *Sylvilagus* spp.

Family Leporidae (Rabbits, Hares)
Size/Weight: approx. 14" long; approx. 1–3 lbs.
Range: Throughout the United States
Habitat: Areas of brush, thickets, grass, or swamps

This genus consists of several species, all called cottontail rabbits, that have various ranges across North America. They are all relatively small, colored gray-brown to reddish brown, with short, white tails (hence the common name), and long ears. Their high rate of reproduction and general abundance make them important food sources for most carnivorous wildlife. Cottontail rabbits are mostly nocturnal but can be seen feeding at almost any time for grasses, herbs, or branches and bark. They never stray too far from brushy cover or their burrows.

Track size (front): 1" wide x 1½" long
Track size (rear): 1" wide x 3" long

Description of Track: There are five toes on the front foot, in an asymmetrical arrangement, but the inner toe is small, raised, and rarely registers in the track. The rear foot has only four toes, all of which show. The claws may or may not register. All pads are reduced, and the sole is covered by dense fur, making an indistinct track. The front track is pointed and the rear track is much longer than wide. Usually the front feet land one in front of the other, not side by side.

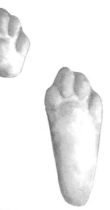

White-tailed Jackrabbit, *Lepus townsendii*

Family Leporidae (Rabbits, Hares)
Size/Weight: approx. 20" long; approx. 7 lbs.
Range: North-central United States, western mountains
Habitat: Prairies, open sageland, mountains

The white-tailed jackrabbit is a large, lanky hare with relatively long legs and huge ears. The color is gray-brown, paler underneath, with a white tail and black-tipped ears. Northern individuals become white in the winter, while others may undergo a more subtle shift to pale gray-brown. The similar, smaller black-tailed jackrabbit has a dark upper surface to the tail. Jackrabbits are mostly nocturnal and solitary, highly alert, and able to elude predators with exceptionally fast runs and high jumps. They forage on grass and other vegetation, but may be limited to bark and buds in winter.

Track size (front): 2" wide x 3" long
Track size (rear): 2½" wide x 5" long
Description of Track: The rear foot is noticeably larger than the front. There are five toes on the front foot, but only four reliably register. The rear foot has four toes. The claws are short and not evident, especially in snow. Toe pads, metacarpal pads, and heel are reduced and concealed by heavy fur, so the track is indistinct. Both tracks have an overall pointy shape, and the rear foot tends to maintain a long, narrow shape without splaying. While bounding, the front feet usually land one in front of the other, not side by side. A well-used trail may be formed between feeding and resting areas.

7

Beaver, *Castor canadensis*
Family Castoridae (Beavers)
Size/Weight: approx. body 28" long, tail 10"; approx. 45 lbs.
Range: Throughout the United States
Habitat: Ponds, lakes, streams with adjacent woodlands

Once nearly extirpated because of hunting and trapping for its pelt, this largest of North American rodents now covers most of its original range. It is heavy and compact with webbed rear feet, large front incisors, and a long, dexterous, scaled, flattened tail. The color is dark brown. Beavers are known for their cooperative construction of impressive dams and lodges made from trees they have felled. Their presence is often indicated by a loud tail slap on the water. Mostly nocturnal, they eat the tender, inner bark of trees as well as small branches and buds.

Track size (front): 3" wide x 3¼" long
Track size (rear): 4½" wide x 6" long
Description of Track: The rear foot is noticeably larger than the front. There are five toes on the front foot, but only four reliably register. The rear foot has five toes. The claws are large and thick, and almost always appear in the track. The palm has fused metacarpal pads, the bumps of which may be more or less noticeable depending on the substrate. The front foot may show a small proximal pad. The heel almost always shows in the rear track, as does the webbing between the toes. Tracks may be obscured by tail drag or by the large rear foot covering the front tracks.

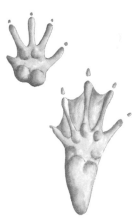

Nutria (Coypu), *Myocastor coypus*
Family Capromyidae (Nutrias)
Size/Weight: approx. 24" long, tail 15"; approx. 3 lbs.
Range: Parts of Pacific, southern, and eastern states
Habitat: Swamps, lakesides

The nutria is a large rodent native to South America that was origi-nally brought to the United States as a source of commercial fur. It is now naturalized in lowland, marshy areas. It has a sausage-shaped body with small ears and a long, round, hairless tail and webbed rear feet. Its fur is yellowish or brownish gray and has a dense, soft undercoat covered by shaggier top hairs. Quite social, nutrias are mostly nocturnal and make burrows in banks at the water's edge. They are excellent swimmers, and they forage for aquatic plants or small aquatic animals.

Track size (front): 1¾" wide x 2" long
Track size (rear): 2½" wide x 4½" long
Description of Track: The rear foot is noticeably larger than the front. The front foot has five toes, the inner one of which is very short but usually registers (at least by the claw mark). All claws are long and sharp and usually register. The rear foot has five thin toes, the outer ones of which can be vague in the track. There are partially fused metacarpal pads, and the front shows two bulbous proximal pads. The rear foot registers a long, thin heel and distal webbing between all toes except the outer two.

Porcupine, *Erethizon dorsatum*
Family Erethizontidae (Porcupines)
Size/Weight: approx. 28" with tail; approx. 18 lbs.
Range: Western and far northeastern United States
Habitat: Forests, thickets

The porcupine is a primarily arboreal, chunky, lackadaisical rodent with small limbs, a bushy tail, and thousands of pointed barbed quills that serve as its only defense. The color is dark brown to blackish. Found alone or in groups, it is mostly nocturnal but can be seen at all times of the day, especially perched in trees. They feed on all types of plant matter, including buds, branches, bark, roots, and leaves.

Track size (front): 1½" wide x 2" long
Track size (rear): 1¾" wide x 3" long
Description of Track: There are four long toes on the front foot and five on the rear, although the smallest, innermost toe may not register. The toes' pads on both feet may be indistinct in the track, but the heavy, long claws are almost always obvious. The fused metacarpal pads form a solid, fleshy mass that has a distinct, pebbly texture. The rear track shows a long, wide heel imprint. Tail drag may be evident, and the usual gait is a slow walk.

Northern Pocket Gopher, *Thomomys talpoides*

Family Geomyidae (Pocket Gophers)
Size/Weight: approx. 12" long with tail; approx. 5 oz.
Range: Inland northern and west-central United States
Habitat: Open woodlands, meadows, mountains

The northern pocket gopher is a compact, mostly subterranean rodent designed for life in earthen tunnels. It has small eyes and ears, a medium-length, sparsely haired tail, and large, exposed front incisors. The feet are relatively large, and the front feet bear long, curved claws for digging. The color is variable shades of brown or gray. Pocket gophers are solitary, active day or night, but can be challenging to see because they tend to stay in their elaborate tunnel systems. In winter, tunnels through the snow collect soil, which shows up as rope-like mounds when the snow melts. Their food consists mostly of plant roots, tubers, and bulbs.

Track size (front): ½" wide x 1" long
Track size (rear): ½" wide x ¾" long (heel not included)
Description of Track: There are five toes on both the front and rear foot, with the inner and outer toes smallest and farther down on the foot. The claws of the front foot are long and pronounced, adding much length to the front track. Metacarpal pads are partly fused. Both feet have additional proximal pads that may register; the rear foot may also show a heel impression. The usual gait is a walk or trot when aboveground.

Pocket Mice, *Perognathus* spp.
Family Heteromyidae (Pocket Mice, Kangaroo Rats)
Size/Weight: approx. 5–7" long with tail; approx. less than 1 oz.
Range: Arid western United States
Habitat: Dry, sandy desert or grasslands
The pocket mice are part of a group of small rodents, so called because of their large cheek pouches (pockets) used to store extra food. They are compact with relatively large heads, long, thin tails, and stronger rear than front feet. Their color ranges from pale grayish to brownish with paler undersides. They are solitary and nocturnal, staying in their burrows during the day, venturing out at night to forage for herbs, seeds, and sometimes insects. They are able to survive without standing water, getting what they need through their foods.

Track size (front): ⅓" wide x ⅓" long
Track size (rear): ⅖" wide x ½" long
Description of Track: Track sizes listed above are averages; different species may vary. Front foot has four toes with a vestigial fifth inner toe that does not usually register. The rear foot has five toes, with the smallest inner toe developed but often not distinct. The claws are fairly long and usually present in the track. Metacarpal pads are fused, and proximal pads are normally obscured by extensive fur on the sole. Pocket mice usually travel in a bound.

Ord's Kangaroo Rat, *Dipodomys ordii*

Family Heteromyidae (Pocket Mice, Kangaroo Rats)
Size/Weight: body approx. 4" long, tail 5½" long; approx. 2 oz.
Range: Inland western United States
Habitat: Lowland prairies and scrublands with sandy soils

One of several species of kangaroo rats across the arid west, the Ord's kangaroo rat occupies the largest range and is one of the smaller varieties. It is a compact rodent with a relatively large head, long tail with a bushy distal portion, and oversize rear feet. Its color is buff to rusty brown with white lateral stripes across the lower body and middle of the tail. Mostly nocturnal and somewhat solitary, kangaroo rats spend the day in their burrows. They hop about, kangaroo-style, foraging for plants, seeds, and insects. They are well adapted to dry conditions, and receive most of the water they need through their food.

Track size (front): ⅖" wide x ½" long
Track size (rear): ¾" wide x 1" long (heel not included)
Description of Track: The rear track is much larger than the front. There are five toes on the front foot, but only four are apparent since the inner fifth toe is highly reduced. There are five toes on the rear foot. The claws are fairly long on the front foot, but quite short on the rear and often not registering. Metatarsal pads are fused with smaller, proximal pads that may or may not register. The rear foot may show the long heel impression, and fur on the sole may obscure the track.

White-footed Mouse, *Peromyscus leucopus*
Family Muridae (Mice)
Size/Weight: approx. 7" long with tail; approx. 1 oz.
Range: Central and eastern United States
Habitat: Quite variable; areas with cover and brush
The white-footed mouse is a very common, small, roundish rodent with a relatively large head, large ears, and a long, thin tail (but not longer than the body length). Its color is brown above and white below, with white feet. They are nocturnal animals, staying in burrows or trees during the day. Quite agile, they are able to bound through dense brush, climb trees, and even swim. They forage for a wide variety of plants, nuts, fruit, or insects.

Track size (front): ⅖" wide x ⅓" long
Track size (rear): ⅖" wide x ⅖" long
Description of Track: There are five toes on the front foot, but the inner toe is vestigial, so only four toes show in the track. The rear foot has five toes, with the three inner toes pointing forward and the outer two facing out. Claws may or may not register. There is a fused metacarpal pad and distinct, round, proximal pads. The sole is hairless, and the heel may or may not register. This track is identical to the very common deer mouse, which occupies much of the same range, but also inhabits the western United States.

Red Squirrel (Pine Squirrel, Chickaree),

Tamiasciurus hudsonicus
Family Sciuridae (Squirrels)
Size/Weight: approx. 12" long with tail; approx. 8 oz.
Range: Northeastern United States, intermountain west
Habitat: coniferous or mixed woodlands

The red squirrel is a feisty, highly territorial squirrel that is most at home in trees. It is relatively small with a bushy tail and large eyes encircled with white. The color is reddish brown above and white below, with a dark band in between. They may be somewhat paler in winter months. Red squirrels are primarily active during the day and at all times of the year. They eat the nuts of pine and spruce cones, but will also eat berries, insects, and mushrooms.

Track size (front): ⁹⁄₁₀" wide x 1" long
Track size (rear): 1" wide x 1¼" long (heel not included)
Description of Track: The front foot has four visible toes, with the inner fifth being greatly reduced. The rear foot has five toes, the outer two of which are lower and to the sides. The thin claws may or may not register. The metacarpal pads are partly fused, and the front foot may also show two round proximal pads. The rear foot has four partly fused pads and a furred heel that sometimes shows. Squirrels generally bound by placing both rear and front feet side by side, compared with mustelids that show front feet one in front of the other.

15

Eastern Gray Squirrel, *Sciurus carolinensis*
Family Sciuridae (Squirrels)
Size/Weight: approx. 18" long with tail; approx. 1¼ lbs.
Range: Eastern United States, isolated areas of Pacific states
Habitat: Mixed hardwood forests

The eastern gray squirrel is a social, arboreal, relatively large squirrel with a long, very bushy tail and large eyes. Its color is gray, sometimes with a brownish cast, whitish below, with pale eye rings. The tail is edged with white-tipped hairs. Active most times of the day, they forage for nuts, fruits, seeds, insects, eggs, and fungi, and may store nuts in ground caches for later eating. They use tree cavities to nest or may build a large nest of twigs and leaves high in a tree.

Track size (front): 1" wide x 1½" long
Track size (rear): 1¼" wide x 2½" long (heel not included)
Description of Track: The front foot has four visible toes, with the inner fifth being greatly reduced. The rear foot has five toes, the outer two of which are lower and to the sides. The thin claws may or may not register. The metacarpal pads are partly fused, and the front foot may also show two round proximal pads. The rear foot has several pads that are distinct, and may show the heel impression. The sole is furless. The gait is a walk or bound, and the bound shows the familiar side-by-side placement of both front and rear feet. The track is similar to the closely related western gray squirrel of the Pacific states.

Southern Flying Squirrel, *Glaucomys volans*
Family Sciuridae (Squirrels)
Size/Weight: approx. 9" long with tail; approx. 3 oz.
Range: Eastern United States
Habitat: Coniferous or deciduous woodlands

The southern flying squirrel is a small, unusual squirrel designed to glide (not fly) from tree to tree or from tree to ground. Flaps of skin connect the front and rear feet, so when outstretched, allow the squirrel to glide over 100 feet and make a delicate landing. The color is grayish-brown, darker along the flanks, and whitish below. They are active at night and are highly social, with several individuals sometimes sharing a nest site in a tree cavity or external structure. They forage for nuts, fruit, insects, fungus, and eggs, and store food in tree cavities for winter use.

Track size (front): ½" wide x ½" long
Track size (rear): ½" wide x 1¼" long (heel included)
Description of Track: The front foot has four visible toes, with the inner fifth being greatly reduced. The rear foot has five toes, the outer two of which are lower and to the sides. The claws are not usually evident in the track. The metacarpal pads are partly fused in both front and rear feet; the front foot may show two additional proximal pads, and the rear foot has a wide arc of the pads and a furred heel. When landing from a glide, flying squirrels make an impression known as the "sitzmark," and bounding continues from there. This species is closely related to the slightly larger northern flying squirrel of mountainous and northern United States.

Eastern Chipmunk, *Tamias striatus*

Family Sciuridae (Squirrels)
Size/Weight: approx. 9" long with tail; approx. 3 oz.
Range: Eastern United States, excluding the far southeast
Habitat: Mixed deciduous woodlands with brush

Along with the similar but smaller least chipmunk, the eastern chipmunk is the most common chipmunk in the United States. It is a small, squirrel-like rodent with a relatively large head and a somewhat bushy tail. Its color is reddish brown with lateral, black and white stripes across the sides and through the face. Solitary, and preferring to stay near brush, rocks, or logs on the ground, chipmunks are also excellent climbers. They forage for nuts, seeds, berries, insects or eggs, and form complex underground tunnel systems where they retreat and store food for the winter.

Track size (front): ⁷⁄₁₀" wide x ⁷⁄₁₀" long
Track size (rear): ¾" wide x ¾" long (heel not included)
Description of Track: The front foot has four visible toes, with an inner fifth toe that is greatly reduced. The rear foot has five toes, the outer two of which are lower and to the sides. The claws may or may not register. The metacarpal pads on the front foot are partly fused, and may also show two round proximal pads. The rear foot has four separate metacarpal pads. The heel is slightly furred and sometimes registers. The common gait is a bound with the front feet landing more or less side by side. The least chipmunk, of the inland west, leaves a similar track but is smaller.

Golden-mantled Ground Squirrel, *Spermophilus lateralis*
Family Sciuridae (Squirrels)
Size/Weight: approx. 10" long with tail; approx. 8 oz.
Range: Mountainous western United States
Habitat: Open coniferous forest, campgrounds
The golden-mantled ground squirrel is one of many types of ground squirrels, all primarily ground-dwelling and able to stand upright on their hind legs with ease. It is shaped somewhat like a chipmunk, with a similar set of lateral, black and white stripes along the sides, but with no head stripes. The overall color is golden-red on the front quarters and grayer on the back and tail, with whitish eye rings. It is more solitary than other ground squirrels and most active during the day. It uses a burrow system to nest and store food, which includes nuts, berries, insects, and eggs. It hibernates for most of the winter.

Track size (front): ¾" wide x ⅖" long
Track size (rear): ¾" wide x ⅘" long (heel not included)
Description of Track: The front foot has four visible toes, with the inner fifth being greatly reduced. The rear foot has five toes, the outer two of which are lower and to the sides. The claws may or may not register. The metacarpal pads on the front foot are partly fused, and may also show two round proximal pads. The pads on the rear foot form a circular pattern. The heel is unfurred and sometimes registers. The bound often shows front feet landing one in front of the other.

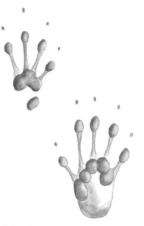

Black-tailed Prairie Dog, *Cynomys ludovicianus*
Family Sciuridae (Squirrels)
Size/Weight: approx. 15" long with tail; approx. 2½ lbs.
Range: West-central United States
Habitat: Arid prairie regions

The black-tailed prairie dog is a large, plump ground squirrel able to stand upright on its hind legs with ease. Its color is pale yellow or buff overall with a black-tipped tail. It has small ears, a short tail, and substantial claws for digging. Diurnal and highly social, prairie dogs create vast burrow systems and mounds in a colony known as a "town." Atop a mound usually perches a sentinel individual, who alerts the colony of danger with a doglike bark. They feed on plant matter and insects, and do not undergo a true hibernation.

Track size (front): 1" wide x 1½" long
Track size (rear): 1¼" wide x 1½" long (heel not included)
Description of Track: The front foot has four visible toes, with the inner fifth being greatly reduced. The rear foot has five toes, the outer two of which are lower and to the sides. The long claws usually register at the tips. The metacarpal pads are partly fused, and the front foot may also show two round proximal pads, one of which is more prominent than the other. The rear foot has several, partly fused pads that are arranged in a long arc. The heel is not furred and may or may not register. The white-tailed prairie dog has a similar track but a more restricted range.

Yellow-bellied Marmot, *Marmota flaviventris*

Family Sciuridae (Squirrels)

Size/Weight: approx. 24" long with tail; approx. 8 lbs. (males larger than females)

Range: Mountainous inland West

Habitat: High-elevation rocky slopes, boulders

The yellow-bellied marmot is a heavy, roundish ground squirrel with a medium-length, somewhat bushy tail and small ears. The thick fur is pale tan-brown overall with a yellowish belly and pale patches on the front of the face. Found alone or in groups, it is active during the day, perching atop boulders or foraging for herbs, grasses, and seeds. It undergoes a long winter hibernation in an underground burrow.

Track size (front): 1¾" wide x 2½" long

Track size (rear): 2" wide x 2½" long (heel not included)

Description of Track: The front foot has four visible toes, with the inner fifth being greatly reduced. The rear foot has five toes, the outer two of which are lower and to the sides. All toes are somewhat narrow, and the claws may or may not register. The metacarpal pads are partly fused, and the front foot may also show two round proximal pads. The rear also has two broad proximal pads and an unfurred heel that may appear in the track. The track is very similar to the slightly smaller groundhog, who occupies a different range.

Groundhog (Woodchuck), *Marmota monax*
Family Sciuridae (Squirrels)
Size/Weight: approx. 22" long with tail; approx. 7 lbs.
Range: Midwest and eastern United States
Habitat: Lowland open woodlands, fields

The groundhog is a large, plump ground squirrel with small ears and a medium-length, somewhat bushy tail. Its thick fur is tawny to grayish with a slightly paler underside and dark feet. Active during the day, they form colonies of extensive, deep burrow systems and use them to quickly escape danger. A sentinel individual may alarm the group by emitting a high-pitched squeal, giving them the colloquial name of "whistle-pig." They eat a variety of grasses and herbs, and hibernate during the winter months.

Track size (front): 1¾" wide x 2¼" long
Track size (rear): 1¾" wide x 2¼" long (heel not included)
Description of Track: The front foot has four visible toes, with the inner fifth being greatly reduced. The rear foot has five toes, the outer two of which are lower and to the sides. Often the length of the toes shows between the digital pads and the palm. The robust, curved claws, designed for digging, are usually obvious. The metacarpal pads are partly fused and lobed, and both feet show two additional proximal pads. The heel of the rear foot is unfurred and may or may not register in the track. Groundhogs are closely related to marmots, whose tracks are slightly larger.

Meadow Jumping Mouse, *Zapus hudsonius*

Family Dipodidae (Jumping Mice)
Size/Weight: approx. 8" long with tail; approx. ¾ oz.
Range: North-central and northeastern United States
Habitat: Woodland areas close to water, meadows

The meadow jumping mouse is a small mouse with large ears, large rear feet, and an extremely long, lightly furred tail (longer than its body length). The color is rusty brown, darker on top, and white below. They are mostly nocturnal but can be seen during the daytime as well. They are excellent swimmers and stay close to stream banks foraging for plants, seeds, and insects. In colder climates they undergo long periods of profound hibernation in underground burrows, where they live on stores of fat.

Track size (front): ½" wide x ⅔" long
Track size (rear): ⅔" wide x ¾" long (heel not included)
Description of Track: The front foot has four visible toes, with the inner fifth being greatly reduced. The rear foot has five toes, with the innermost being quite short and low on the foot. All toes are long and thin, and claws are most likely to register on the rear foot. The metacarpal pads on the front foot are partly fused but still distinct, and there are two round proximal pads that may or may not show. The rear foot has separate pads and sometimes shows the long, thin heel impression. Track is very similar to the woodland jumping mouse.

Bushy-tailed Woodrat, *Neotoma cinerea*

Family Cricetidae (Voles, Woodrats, Muskrats)

Size/Weight: approx. 14" long with tail; approx. 12 oz. (males larger than females)

Range: Western United States

Habitat: Mixed woodlands, rocky riparian areas

Also known as the packrat, the bushy-tailed woodrat is a sturdy rodent with large ears and a long, distinct, bushy tail. Its color is pale brown with some long, darker hairs above, and whitish below. It is solitary and nocturnal, though it can be seen during the day as well. An excellent climber, it may forage in trees or on the ground for plants, seeds, fruits, and insects. It is readily attracted to shiny objects and will hoard them in caches.

Track size (front): ¾" wide x ¾" long

Track size (rear): ⅘" wide x 1¼" long (heel not included)

Description of Track: The front foot has four visible toes, with the inner fifth being greatly reduced but sometimes registering as a small mark. The rear foot has five toes, the inner of which is quite small. The toe pads may show a constricted area near the middle, and the claws are not usually evident in the track. The front foot has partly fused metacarpal pads and two round proximal pads, while the pads of the rear foot are distinct. The long, thin heel may or may not register.

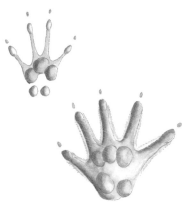

Muskrat, *Ondata zibethicus*
Family Cricetidae (Voles, Woodrats, Muskrats)
Size/Weight: approx. 22" long with tail; approx. 3 lbs.
Range: Throughout the United States except for far southern regions
Habitat: Wetland and riparian areas

The muskrat is a plump, well-furred, semi-aquatic rodent with characteristics of both a large rat and a beaver. The long tail is mostly hairless with scales and somewhat flattened along the sides to aid in swimming. The color is deep brown to blackish with dense, waterproof hair underneath and coarser guard hairs on the outside. Muskrats may be seen most times of the day, swimming and foraging for aquatic plants and small aquatic animals. They burrow into banks or build a conical lodge of sticks and mud.

Track size (front): 1¼" wide x 1½" long
Track size (rear): 2" wide x 2" long
Description of Track: The rear track is substantially larger than the front. The front foot has four visible toes, with the inner fifth being greatly reduced and not evident. The rear foot has five toes that are bordered by stiff hairs that can leave a ridge-like impression next to the toes. The claws are long, for digging, and are usually apparent in the track, especially on the front foot. All toes are somewhat narrow. The metacarpal pads are partly fused, and the front foot may also show two round proximal pads. The rear also has two broad proximal pads. Note the lack of webbing between toes, unlike that of the larger beaver.

Voles, *Microtus* spp.
Family Cricetidae (Voles, Woodrats, Muskrats)
Size/Weight: approx. 5–8" long with tail; approx. 1–5 oz.
Range: Throughout the United States
Habitat: Grasslands, meadows

The voles include many species of small, compact, roundish, mouse-like rodents with relatively short, lightly haired tails and small eyes and ears. Their color is varying shades of brown or gray with lighter undersides. Active most times, day or night, they utilize burrow networks that they build themselves or that other rodents species have made. They forage mostly for tender plant foliage or roots and tubers from underground.

Track size (front): ⅖" wide x ⅖" long
Track size (rear): ⅖" wide x ½" long
Description of Track: The front foot has four visible toes, with the inner fifth being greatly reduced and not evident. The rear foot has five toes, the outer two of which are low on the foot and to the sides, and which may leave an impression along the entire length of the toe. Claws may or may not register. The metacarpal pads are partly fused and lobed, and the front foot may also show two round proximal pads. The rear foot has more distinct, unfused metacarpal pads and a long heel that sometimes leaves an impression. Tracks of all voles are among the smallest in our region.

Coyote, *Canis latrans*

Family Canidae (Coyotes, Wolves, Foxes)
Size/Weight: body approx. 3' long without tail; approx. 35 lbs.
Range: Throughout the United States
Habitat: Open country, scrub, grasslands

The coyote is an intelligent and adaptable canid that has been able to survive in a wide variety of habitats and through persecution by humans. It looks like an average-size dog with a long, thin muzzle and pointed ears. The color can range from gray to light brown or reddish. It has a bushy tail that is held low or between the legs. Coyotes hunt alone or in small packs, primarily during the night. Their diet is varied, and they scavenge for about anything edible, including rodents, rabbits, snakes, berries, insects, or carrion.

Track size (front): 2½" wide x 3" long
Track size (rear): 2" wide x 2½" long
Description of Track: The front track is larger than the rear. Both feet have four toes that are visible in the track and a small dewclaw high on the foot that does not usually register. Claws are close to the ends of the toes, although the outside claws are not always clear. The metatarsal pads are fused and lobed into a somewhat triangular shape, and smaller on the rear foot. Being digitigrade, the heel does not contact the ground. Compared to the coyote, domestic dog tracks are similar but tend to be rounder and looser in structure.

Gray Wolf, *Canis lupus*

Family Canidae (Coyotes, Wolves, Foxes)

Size/Weight: approx. body 4½' long without tail; approx. 90 lbs. (males larger than females)

Range: Alaska, scattered areas of northern Rocky Mountains, Yellowstone Park

Habitat: Forests; tundra in northern range

Also known as the timber wolf, the gray wolf was once found throughout the western United States but is now restricted to small wilderness areas in this country. It is our largest canid, and is colored varying combinations of black, gray, reddish, or even white in the north. Wolves live and travel in packs with a tight social structure, and hunt large game such as elk and caribou, or small mammals to mouse-size. Territory and communication are conveyed through their piercing howls and urine marks.

Track size (front): 4" wide x 4½" long
Track size (rear): 3½" wide x 4" long

Description of Track: The front track is larger than the rear. Both feet have four toes that are visible in the track and arranged symmetrically, and a small dewclaw high on the foot that does not usually register. Claws are large and appear close to the ends of the toes. The metatarsal pads are fused and lobed into a somewhat triangular shape, and smaller on the rear foot. Being digitigrade, the heel does not contact the ground. The track is similar to the coyote but much larger.

Gray Fox, *Urocyon cinereoargenteus*
Family Canidae (Coyotes, Wolves, Foxes)
Size/Weight: approx. body 3' long with tail; approx. 10 lbs.
Range: Most of the United States except northwest and north-central states
Habitat: Open woodlands, chaparral
The gray fox is a small, stealthy, nimble canid with a bushy tail and the ability to climb trees using its short, curved, retractable claws. Its fur is gray and white speckled above, reddish along the sides and legs, and there is a black streak down the back and tail, ending in a black tail tip. The muzzle is thin and small, while the ears are comparatively large. They are mostly solitary and nocturnal, and feed on a varied diet including rabbits, rodents, insects, nuts, and fruit.

Track size (front): 1½" wide x 1¾" long
Track size (rear): 1½" wide x 1⅔" long
Description of Track: The front track is larger than the rear and overall round in shape. Both feet have four toes that are visible in the track and a small dewclaw high on the foot that does not usually register. The small, semi-retractable claws do not normally register. The metatarsal pads are fused and lobed into a somewhat triangular shape and are smaller on the rear foot. Being digitigrade, the heel does not contact the ground. Compared to the gray fox, the tracks of other canids are similar but larger in size.

Red Fox, *Vulpes vulpes*
Family Canidae (Coyotes, Wolves, Foxes)
Size/Weight: approx. body 38" long with tail; approx. 12 lbs.
Range: Most of the United States except parts of the west and southwest
Habitat: Open woodlands, fields, brushy areas; may approach urban centers
Like other foxes, the red fox is a wily, secretive, adaptable, dog-like mammal with a small muzzle, large ears, and a bushy tail. It is rusty-red above, white or gray below, with black "stockings" on the legs and a white-tipped tail. Color variations may include black, slate-gray, or with a dark cross along the shoulders.

Track size (front): 1¾" wide x 2¼" long
Track size (rear): 1½" wide x 2" long
Description of Track: The front track is larger than the rear, over-all round in shape, and somewhat symmetrical. Both feet have four toes that are visible in the track and a small dewclaw high on the foot that does not usually register. The small, semi-retractable claws may or may not register. The metatarsal pads are fused and lobed into a somewhat triangular shape and are smaller on the rear foot, and there is a prominent, shallow V-shaped ridge across the pad. The sole of the foot is furred, making the area between the pads obscure. Being digitigrade, the heel does not contact the ground.

Kit Fox, *Vulpes macrotis*

Family Canidae (Coyotes, Wolves, Foxes)
Size/Weight: approx. body 28" long with tail; approx. 4 lbs.
Range: Southwestern United States
Habitat: Sandy desert areas, prairies, sagebrush

Our smallest canid, and the only one found in desert regions, the kit fox is a diminutive, house cat–size fox with comparatively large ears and a delicate face. Its color is pale reddish-brown mottled with gray above, and lighter below. The tail has a black tip. It is primarily nocturnal, hunting for small mammals, insects, and reptiles, but it will also take carrion if available. It retreats to a den or burrow during the day. Some consider the kit fox to be the same species as the slightly larger swift fox of the Great Plains.

Track size (front): 1¼" wide x 1½" long
Track size (rear): 1⅕" wide x 1⅖" long
Description of Track: The front track is larger than the rear, overall round in shape, and somewhat symmetrical. Both feet have four toes that are visible in the track and a small dewclaw high on the foot that does not usually register. The small, delicate claws may or may not register. The metatarsal pads are fused and lobed into a somewhat triangular shape. The sole of the foot is furred, making the area between the pads obscure. Being digitigrade, the heel does not contact the ground. The track is similar to other canids but much smaller.

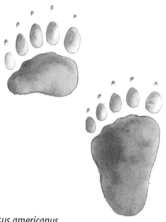

Black Bear, *Ursus americanus*

Family Ursidae (Bears)

Size/Weight: approx. 3′ tall at shoulder, 6′ tall standing; up to 600 lbs. (male larger than female)

Range: Northern United States, Alaska, and other scattered mountains regions

Habitat: Forests, open range

Although the smallest bear in North America, the black bear is still a heavy, lumbering bear with thick (but not humped) shoulders, short legs, and small ears and tail. Its color ranges from black to cinnamon or even blue-gray or white in its extreme northern range. The muzzle is always colored brownish. It feeds mostly at night, covering large areas of land for plants, roots, berries, grubs, and occasionally small animals, fish, and carrion. It is usually solitary except in mating season or in family units of cubs and a mother, and spends most of the winter hibernating in a den, but can be aroused quickly.

Track size (front): 6″ wide x 7″ long

Track size (rear): 6″ wide x 9″ long

Description of Track: There are five toes on each foot, with the smallest, inside toe often being quite faint. The claws are long and may or may not register, and the palm is large and composed of fused metacarpal pads. Bears are plantigrade, meaning that they walk on the full foot including the heel, and this is evident on the rear foot but rarely on the front.

Grizzly Bear, *Ursus arctos horribilis*

Family Ursidae (Bears)

Size/Weight: approx. 3½' tall at shoulder, 7' long; up to 800 lbs.

Range: Rocky Mountains, Alaska

Habitat: Remote, high mountains, tundra in the far north

The grizzly bear is a subspecies of the brown bear that once roamed most of western North America, but is now restricted to wilderness areas where they are protected by law. It is a large, powerful bear with a distinctive hump above the shoulder blades and a rounded, "dished" face. The thick fur is brown to golden brown, tipped with silver that gives a frosted, grizzled appearance. They are mostly solitary but will congregate around food sources like heavy runs of salmon, upon which they gorge. They also eat berries, plants, grubs, and mammals to the size of bison or moose. In the winter they undergo a light hibernation, or torpor.

Track size (front): 5" wide x 5½" long

Track size (rear): 6" wide x 10" long

Description of Track: There are five toes on each foot, with slight webbing between them on the front foot. The claws are straight and very long, even longer than toe length. The palm is large and composed of fused metacarpal pads. Bears are plantigrade, meaning that they walk on the full foot including the heel, and this is evident on the rear foot but only partially on the front.

33

Ringtail, *Bassariscus astutus*
Family Procyonidae (Ringtails, Raccoons)
Size/Weight: approx. 30" long with tail; approx. 2 lbs.
Range: Southwest United States, California
Habitat: Rocky deserts, forests

The ringtail is a small, secretive mammal with delicate features, big, dark eyes, and a long, bushy tail. Although sometimes referred to as the ringtail cat, it is not related to cats but allied more with raccoons. Its color is light brown above, paler below, with a striped black and white tail. Mostly nocturnal, it is usually found alone or in pairs. Ringtails are very agile climbers, using their long tails and flexible ankles to navigate through trees and rocks. They forage for both plants and animals with a diet that includes berries, insects, birds, and small mammals.

Track size (front): 1" wide x 1¼" long
Track size (rear): 1" wide x 1¼" long
Description of Track: There are five toes on each foot, and the smallest, inside toe does not always register. The claws are short and semi-retractable, and may or may not register. The metacarpal pads are fused and lobed and appear in an arc, and that of the rear foot is quite long. On the front foot there is a small proximal pad.

Raccoon, *Procyon lotor*

Family Procyonidae (Ringtails, Raccoons)
Size/Weight: approx. 34" long with tail; approx. 20 lbs.
Range: Most of the United States except parts of high western mountains
Habitat: woodlands, streams or lakesides, urban areas

The raccoon is a highly adaptable mammal, equally at home in remote forests or urban centers. It is stocky and heavy with a short, masked face and a bushy coat. Its color is pale gray mixed with black, with a tail ringed black and gray. Incredibly dexterous fingers allow it to undo knots and even work doorknobs. Raccoons are primarily nocturnal and may be seen alone or in small groups. They prefer to feed near a water source, often dipping their food in water first, and will eat just about anything, including fruits, nuts, insects, fish, crayfish, and worms.

Track size (front): 2½" wide x 2½" long
Track size (rear): 2¼" wide x 3½" long (including heel)
Description of Track: There are five toes on each foot, all of which register, and are bulbous and continuous with the palm. The claws are short and nonretractable, usually leaving small dots in the track. The metacarpal pads are fused, form an acute arc, and are continuous with the surrounding flesh of the foot. The rear track shows the impression of the broad heel. The track is virtually symmetrical and resembles the handprint of a small child.

Badger, *Taxidea taxus*
Family Mustelidae (Mustelids)
Size/Weight: approx. 24" long with tail; approx. 20 lbs.
Range: Western and midwestern United States
Habitat: Grasslands, desert

The badger is a compact, tough mustelid with a short tail and very long claws, especially on the front feet. It is densely furred and colored pale gray-brown with a white or buff belly and black feet. It has a white stripe through the forehead and over the head, and a white and black patterned face. Badgers are solitary and nocturnal, though are often visible during early morning hours. They use their strong, clawed feet to excavate rodent burrows for the prey therein, and will also eat reptiles and birds. In cold climates they hibernate in underground burrows.

Track size (front): 2" wide x 3" long
Track size (rear): 1¾" wide x 2" long (not including heel)
Description of Track: The front foot is noticeably larger than the rear. There are five toes on each foot, although the smaller inner toes do not always register. The claws are long, heavy, and prominent in the track. The metacarpal pads are fused in a loose arc shape, with an additional proximal pad in the front foot and a faint heel impression on the rear. The sole is not furry as in most other mustelids.

Mink, *Mustela vison* or *Neovison vison*
Family Mustelidae (Mustelids)
Size/Weight: approx. 20" long with tail; approx. 2½ lbs.
Range: Most of the United States except for western and southwestern states
Habitat: Areas near streams and lakes

The mink is an elongate, short-legged mustelid with a long tail, webbed feet, and a semi-aquatic lifestyle. Its luxurious pelt is dark, blackish-brown, sometimes has a whitish area around the mouth, and may have pale spotting on the underside. Minks are mostly nocturnal and solitary, are excellent swimmers, and never stray too far from a water source. They are carnivores, eating aquatic animals and invertebrates, but will also take birds, eggs, and rabbits.

Track size (front): 1½" wide x 1¾" long
Track size (rear): 1½" wide x 1½" long

Description of Track: There are five toes on each foot, although the smaller inner toes do not always register. The toes, especially on the front foot, often splay apart, and webbing between the toes may be evident in the track. The medium-length claws may or may not register. The metacarpal pads are fused in a loose arc shape, with an additional proximal pad in the front foot.

Long-tailed Weasel and Short-tailed Weasel,
Mustela frenata and *Mustela erminea*
Family Mustelidae (Mustelids)
Size/Weight: approx. 14" long with tail; approx. 6 oz. (long-tail larger than short-tail)
Range: Throughout the United States (long-tail), northern and western United States (short-tail)
Habitat: Variety of habitats with cover, often near water

These species have a similar track and are both small, elongate, long-necked, wily predators. The long-tailed weasel is reddish-brown with buff underparts and throat, with a black tip to its long tail. The short-tailed weasel (also known as the ermine) has a shorter tail and is colored similarly except for its white feet. In winter, the short-tailed weasel becomes white except for the tail tip. Both are nocturnal and solitary, are excellent climbers, and due to their shape can slip into burrows to attack rodents living within. They also hunt rabbits, birds, eggs, and fish.

Track size (front): ¾" wide x ¾" long
Track size (rear): ¾" wide x ¾" long (not including heel)
Description of Track: There are five toes on each foot, although the smaller inner toes do not always register. The claws usually register. The metacarpal pads are fused in a triangular shape, with an additional proximal pad in the front foot and a faint heel impression on the rear. The sole is furred, resulting in an obscure definition of the track. Long-tailed weasel tracks are slightly larger than those of the short-tailed weasel, but both are quite small.

Black-footed Ferret, *Mustela nigripes*

Family Mustelidae (Mustelids)
Size/Weight: approx. 21" long with tail; approx. 2¼ lbs.
Range: Isolated areas of west-central United States
Habitat: Prairies

The black-footed ferret is a rare and endangered species whose populations have diminished due to the extermination of its favored food, the prairie dog. It is shaped like a large weasel with an elongate body, long neck and tail, short legs, and small ears. It is colored pale golden-brown with black feet, tail tip, and facial mask. Ferrets are mostly nocturnal and solitary, and hunt prairie dogs by slinking into their burrows.

Track size (front): 1¼" wide x 1¼" long
Track size (rear): 1¼" wide x 1¼" long (not including heel)
Description of Track: There are five toes on each foot, although the smaller inner toes do not always register. The medium-length claws may or may not register. The metacarpal pads are fused in a loose arc shape or triangle, with an additional proximal pad in the front foot and a faint, long heel impression on the rear. The foot is quite furry and may make for a fuzzy, indistinct track. Ferret tracks are similar in shape but larger than those of weasels.

Fisher, *Martes pennanti*

Family Mustelidae (Mustelids)

Size/Weight: approx. 34" long with tail; approx. 9 lbs.

Range: Far northern United States, Rocky Mountains, mountainous parts of California

Habitat: Forested areas

The fisher is basically weasel-shaped with an elongate body, short legs, and a long, bushy tail, but heavier and thicker. Its fur is dense and colored a rich, dark brown tipped with white, giving a grizzled or frosted, glistening appearance. Its range has been severely reduced due to hunting for its pelt. Fishers are solitary animals, active day or night, excellent climbers, and agile predators among thick forests and fallen timber. They hunt a wide variety of mammals and birds, even preying upon porcupines. They will also eat plants, berries, or carrion. Contrary to its common name, they rarely feed on fish.

Track size (front): 3" wide x 3¼" long

Track size (rear): 3" wide x 2¾" long

Description of Track: There are five toes on each foot, although the smaller inner toes do not always register. The claws are short and retractable, and may or may not register. The metacarpal pads are fused in a loose arc shape, with an additional proximal pad in the front foot. A heel impression does not occur.

Marten, *Martes americana*
Family Mustelidae (Mustelids)
Size/Weight: approx. 25" long with tail; approx. 2 lbs.
Range: Far northern United States, south into Rocky Mountains and mountainous California
Habitat: Forested areas

The marten is an elongate, slender mustelid with a long tail, short legs, and pointed snout. It is stockier than a weasel with larger, rounded ears, but much smaller than a fisher, with whom it shares a similar range. Its color is golden-brown with a buff or orange patch on the throat and chest. Numbers of this species have been severely reduced by trappers for its luxurious pelt. Martens are nocturnal and solitary. Adept climbers, they hunt small mammals in trees or on the ground, and may also feed on nuts and berries when available.

Track size (front): 2" wide x 2¼" long
Track size (rear): 2" wide x 2" long (not including heel)
Description of Track: There are five toes on each foot, although the smaller inner toes do not always register. The claws are short, and may or may not register. The metacarpal pads are fused in a loose arc shape, with an additional proximal pad in the front foot and a faint heel impression on the rear. The sole is heavily furred, creating an indistinct track, especially on the rear foot.

Wolverine, *Gulo gulo*
Family Mustelidae (Mustelids)
Size/Weight: approx. 38" long with tail; approx. 30 lbs. (males larger than females)
Range: Northern Rocky Mountains, mountainous California, Alaska
Habitat: High-altitude forest, tundra

The wolverine is a powerful predator and the largest member of the mustelid family. At first glance it may be mistaken for a bear cub, with its large feet, thick fur, and bushy tail. Their color is dark brown, with pale, lateral stripes that run from the shoulders to the rump. There is also a pale patch between the eyes and the ears. Wolverines are reclusive and solitary, at home on the ground or climbing trees, and they are capable of killing animals much larger than themselves, although they commonly eat carrion and berries when available.

Track size (front): 4" wide x 4½" long
Track size (rear): 4" wide x 4½" long (not including heel)
Description of Track: There are five toes on each foot, although the smaller inner toes do not always register. The claws are fairly short, and may or may not register. The metacarpal pads are fused in a loose arc shape, with an additional proximal pad in the front foot and a faint heel impression on the rear. There is a variable amount of fur on the sole—greater in winter—that may obscure the definition of the track.

River Otter, *Lontra canadensis*
Family Mustelidae (Mustelids)

Size/Weight: approx. 4' long with tail; approx. 20 lbs.

Range: Throughout the United States except parts of the southwest and midwest

Habitat: Areas near streams, lakes, or estuaries

The river otter is a large, curious, and playful mustelid with a mostly aquatic lifestyle. It is elongate and sinuous, with small ears, webbed feet, and a long, somewhat thickened tail to aid in swimming. Its fur is thick, dark brown above and pale gray below and across the lower face. River otters are social and often travel in small family groups. They hunt primarily in the water for fish, amphibians, or aquatic invertebrates. They live in burrows near water and form well-used trails along the shore or between water sources.

Track size (front): 2½" wide x 2¾" long
Track size (rear): 3" wide x 3¼" long (not including heel)

Description of Track: The rear foot is noticeably larger than the front. There are five toes on each foot, with extensive webbing between the toes, being most evident on the rear foot. The claws are short and may or may not register. The metacarpal pads are fused in a loose arc shape, with an additional proximal pad in the front foot and a faint heel impression on the rear. The sole is not heavily furred. There is often noticeable tail drag between the tracks, and long, deep impressions where otters have decided to slide, especially downhill.

Striped Skunk, *Mephitis mephitis*
Family Mephitidae (skunks)
Size/Weight: approx. 22" long with tail; approx. 8 lbs.
Range: Throughout the United States
Habitat: Woodlands, rocky areas, usually near a water source

The striped skunk is known primarily for its ability to elude danger by spraying a noxious fluid from an anal duct. It is a stocky, weasel-like mammal with a long, bushy tail and long front claws for digging. Its color is black with broad white stripes running down its sides, merging at a white stripe on the upper part of the tail. Usually solitary, striped skunks stay in dens during the day and forage at night. Being omnivorous, they will eat a wide variety of foods including fruit, nuts, insects, small mammals, and eggs.

Track size (front): 1" wide x 1½" long
Track size (rear): 1" wide x 2" long

Description of Track: There are five toes on each foot, tightly spaced, and the smaller inner toes do not always register. The claws are long and curved on the front foot, shorter on the rear, and prominent in the track. The metacarpal pads are fused in a loose arc shape, with an additional proximal pad in the front foot and a separate heel pad on the rear. The sole is hairless. The print is relatively small for the size of the animal, and it stays compact with toes that rarely splay apart.

Eastern Spotted Skunk and Western Spotted Skunk,

Spilogale putorious and *Spilogale gracilis*
Family Mephitidae (skunks)
Size/Weight: approx. 18" long with tail; approx. 1½ lbs.
Range: Western United States (western spotted skunk); Great Plains and southeastern United States (eastern spotted skunk)
Habitat: Brushy open woodlands, grasslands; usually near water

These closely related skunks are smaller than the striped skunk and share its ability to spray a noxious liquid in defense from ducts near the anus. They are weasel-like with thick, bushy tails, fine, soft fur, and long claws. Their color is black with variable and irregular white spotting and striping on the head and back, with a white-tipped tail. The eastern species has more extensive white markings. Solitary and nocturnal, they stay in dens during the day. They can climb trees but mostly forage on the ground for a variety of prey including fruit, insects, small mammals, birds, and eggs.

Track size (front): 1" wide x 1¼" long
Track size (rear): ⅘" wide x 2" long
Description of Track: There are five toes on each foot, and the smaller inner toes do not always register. The claws are long on the front foot, slightly shorter on the rear, and prominent in the track. The metacarpal pads are fused with clear lobes, arranged in a loose arc shape, with additional proximal pads on the front foot and a separate, cleaved heel pad on the rear. The print stays compact with toes that rarely splay apart.

Mountain Lion (Cougar), *Puma concolor*
Family Felidae (cats)
Size/Weight: approx. body 7' long, tail 2½' long; approx. 125 lbs. (males larger than females)
Range: Throughout western United States; sporadic in the east and Florida
Habitat: Open to dense woodlands, brush, cliffs

The mountain lion is a reclusive, huge, powerful cat with a long tail that requires a very large territorial range. Its fur is a blend of tawny browns, tans, and grays, with a paler underside and white on the chest and throat. The tail tip is dark brown, as are the backs of the ears and marks on the muzzle. They are mostly solitary except during breeding season or when with kittens. They hunt by stealth: waiting on a rocky ledge or tree, or by slinking through grass to ambush their prey, which includes deer, elk, or smaller mammals.

Track size (front): 3¼" wide x 3¼" long
Track size (rear): 3¼" wide x 3" long
Description of Track: The front track is larger than the rear. Both feet have four toes that are visible in the track and a small dewclaw high on the foot that does not usually register. The track is arranged asymmetrically, with the outer three toes in an arc; the third toe from the outside being farthest forward. Claws are retractable and do not normally register. The metacarpal pads are fused and lobed into a somewhat trapezoidal shape, with two lobes on the leading edge and three on the trailing edge. The front track is wider than the rear, and the toes on cats splay easily, making the track appear even wider.

Bobcat, *Lynx rufus* or *Felis rufus*
Family Felidae (cats)

Size/Weight: approx. body 28" long, tail 5" long, approx. 22 lbs.
Range: Throughout the United States except parts of the midwest
Habitat: A wide variety of habitats, including forests, riparian areas, chaparral

The bobcat is about double the size of a housecat, is well-camouflaged, and has a very short, "bobbed" tail. Its face appears wide due to the long hair tufts below the ears, and the ears are tipped with short, black hairs. Its color is light brown to reddish above, pale or whitish below, and spotted with dark brown or black that sometimes becomes streaked on the legs. The tail is striped, and black along the top edge. Movements of the bobcat are typically during early morning hours and after dusk, except in winter when they will be active during the day. They hunt by stealth, ambushing their favored prey of rabbits, other small mammals, and birds.

Track size (front): 2" wide x 2" long
Track size (rear): 1⅘" wide x 2¼" long
Description of Track: Both feet have four toes that are visible in the track and a small dewclaw high on the foot that does not usually register. The track is arranged asymmetrically, with the outer three toes in an arc; the third toe from the outside being farthest forward. Claws are retractable and do not normally register. The metacarpal pads are fused and lobed into a somewhat trapezoidal shape, with two lobes on the leading edge and three on the trailing edge. The front track is wider than the rear, and the toes on cats splay easily, making the track appear even wider. Similar to the mountain lion tracks but much smaller.

Canada Lynx, *Lynx canadensis*
Family Felidae (cats)
Size/Weight: approx. body 34" long, tail 4" long; approx. 20 lbs.
Range: Scattered regions of the northwest and Rocky Mountains
Habitat: Mountainous forests

The Canada lynx is slightly larger than the bobcat and with a more northerly and limited range in the United States. It is pale brownish-gray overall, lighter below, with subtle darker spotting or streaking. The tail is very short (bobbed) and has an entirely black tip. Long fur about the neck forms a ruff and makes the head seem quite wide, and the pointed ears end in long, black tufts. Mostly nocturnal and solitary, Canada lynx stealthily stalk their prey, then make a quick and sudden attack. Prey is mostly snowshoe hares, but also includes other small mammals and birds.

Track size (front): 4" wide x 3¾" long
Track size (rear): 3½" wide x 3½" long
Description of Track: The front track is larger than the rear. Both feet have four toes that are visible in the track and a small dewclaw high on the foot that does not usually register. The track is arranged asymmetrically, with the outer three toes in an arc; the third toe from the outside being farthest forward. Claws are retractable and do not normally register. The metatarsal pads are fused and lobed into a somewhat trapezoidal shape, and heavy furring on the sole makes the pad appear small and often leaves an impression across the whole track. The front track is wider than the rear, and the toes on cats can splay apart widely, giving extra flotation in deep snow.

White-tailed Deer, *Odocoileus virginianus*

Family Cervidae (deer, elk, moose)

Size/Weight: approx. body 6' long, tail 10" long; approx. 140 lbs. (males larger than females)

Range: Throughout United States except parts of west-central states

Habitat: Dense forest, forest edges, swamps

Our smallest deer, the white-tailed deer is a secretive mammal of thick forests, is very agile, fast, and able to outmaneuver most predators once spotted. The male has antlers with a main beam that supports smaller prongs which grow from it. The color of its fur is slate-gray in winter and reddish-brown in summer, with a white belly and throat. When alarmed, it raises its tail, revealing the brilliant white underside, hence its colloquial name of "flag-tail." White-tailed deer travel in small groups in summer, but in winter may congregate in larger herds. Being herbivores, they forage for grasses, herbs, and nuts.

Track size (front): 2" wide x 3" long
Track size (rear): 1½" wide x 2½" long

Description of Track: The front track is larger than the rear. Both feet have four toes, with two hooved inner toes and two outer dewclaws that do not register in the track. The track is shaped like an inverted heart and is taller than wide. There is a thin ridge of subunguinis, and a noticeable ridge between the hooves. The shape is almost identical to the mule deer but smaller.

Mule Deer, *Odocoileus hemionus*

Family Cervidae (deer, elk, moose)

Size/Weight: body approx. 6' long with tail; approx. 120–350 lbs. (males larger than females)

Range: Western United States

Habitat: Quite variable; forests, chaparral, bushy grasslands

The mule deer is common throughout its range and is so called because of its very large, mule-like ears. Its color is gray-brown in winter, rusty brown in summer, with a white throat, muzzle, and belly. The tail has a black tip in Rocky Mountain populations, while those of the northwest have tails with a black top surface. Males have antlers that are evenly forked, not with tines from a central beam (as in the white-tail deer). In summer, the antlers are covered in velvet. They are active at twilight hours, moving in small groups or singly, browsing for tree branches, grasses, and herbs.

Track size (front): 2¼" wide x 3¼" long

Track size (rear): 2" wide x 3" long

Description of Track: The front track is larger than the rear. Both feet have four toes, with two hooved inner toes and two outer dewclaws that do not register in the track. The track is shaped like an inverted heart and is taller than wide. There is a thin ridge of subunguinis and a noticeable ridge between the hooves. The shape is almost identical to the white-tail deer but larger. The gait is often a "stot" or "pronk," a bounding run where all four feet hit the ground together.

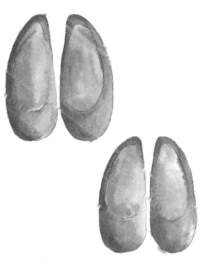

Elk (Wapiti), *Cervus elaphus*
Family Cervidae (deer, elk, moose)
Size/Weight: body approx. 8' long, tail 4" long; males to 800 lbs., females to 500 lbs.
Range: Rocky Mountains, far northwestern United States
Habitat: Mountainous forests, high meadows

The elk is a large, gregarious member of the deer family with a pale, stubby tail. Its fur is short in the summer, longer in the winter, and colored pale rusty-brown with a darker neck and face. The rump is buff, surrounded by dark brown. Males have a shaggy, dark mane about the neck and large antlers with tines growing from a central beam. Usually active in the morning and evening, elk form large flocks of up to hundreds of individuals. They browse for grass, herbs, branches, and the tender inner bark of trees.

Track size (front): 3½" wide x 5" long
Track size (rear): 3¼" wide x 4½" long
Description of Track: The front track is larger than the rear. Both feet have four toes, with two hooved inner toes and two outer dewclaws that do not register in the track. The track is shaped like an inverted heart and is taller than wide. The shape is much broader at the tips than the tracks of other deer, and the toe pads only occupy a small portion of the trailing edge of the track.

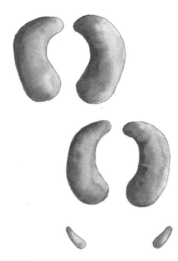

Caribou (Reindeer), *Rangifer tarandus*

Family Cervidae (deer, elk, moose)

Size/Weight: body approx. 6′ long; approx. 250 lbs. (males larger than females)

Range: Northern Rocky Mountains, Alaska

Habitat: Mountainous forests and meadow, tundra in the northern regions

The caribou is a stocky, heavy member of the deer family, but smaller than an elk. The fur color can vary considerably but is generally pale to dark brown with a whitish, maned neck, rump, and feet just above the hooves. Both males and females grow antlers (those of the male being larger), with a rear portion that supports the tines and a front portion that is palmately pointed. The tail is short and stubby. Caribou often form huge flocks, especially in migration, and are mostly herbivorous, feeding on grasses, lichens, and branches.

Track size (front): 5″ wide x 4″ long

Track size (rear): 4″ wide x 3½″ long (not including dewclaws)

Description of Track: Both feet have four toes, with two hooved inner toes and two outer, well-developed dewclaws that often register in the track. The track is very broad and round, wider than long, with much space between the hooves, and resembles two crescents facing each other. The broad foot and dewclaws help with flotation and traction in deep snow.

Moose, *Alces alces*
Family Cervidae (deer, elk, moose)
Size/Weight: body approx. 8 ½' long; approx. 800 lbs. or more (males larger than females)
Range: Northern Rocky Mountains, Alaska
Habitat: Moist or marshy woodlands

The moose is the largest member of the deer family, and second only to the bison in size of North American mammals. It has long, thin legs, a broad, drooping snout, and a hanging tuft of hair below the throat called a "bell." Males have huge, palmate antlers that grow to 5 feet across. The color is brown overall with pale gray legs. Usually found alone or in small family groups, moose are herbivores that graze on woody twigs and branches, or aquatic plants.

Track size (front): 4" wide x 6" long
Track size (rear): 3¾" wide x 5½" long
Description of Track: The front track is larger than the rear. Both feet have four toes, with two hooved inner toes and two outer dew-claws that do not register in the track, except in deep substrate. The track is very large, narrow, and pointed in front and rounded in back, with a noticeable, narrow subunguinis ridge inside of the hoof wall. Hooves may splay apart, making the track wider.

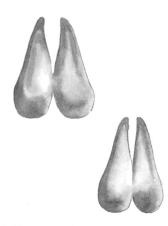

Pronghorn, *Antilocapra americana*
Family Antilocapridae (pronghorn)
Size/Weight: body approx. 4½' long; approx. 120 lbs. (males larger than females)
Range: Western United States
Habitat: Grassy plains, sagebrush

The pronghorn is the only member of its family and bears a resemblance to the antelopes of the Old World. It is colored light brown with a white rump patch, belly, and band about the neck. The neck also has a darker brown band and dark facial patterning. Both sexes have rough, black, flattened horns, which curve at the tip and have a single, forward-projecting prong. The outer sheath of the horn is shed and regrown each year. Pronghorns are primarily active during the morning and afternoon, are found singly or in small groups, and forage on grasses, herbaceous plants, and sagebrush. When pursued they can run up to 40 mph, making them the fastest mammals in North America.

Track size (front): 2¼" wide x 2¾" long
Track size (rear): 1¾" wide x 2½" long
Description of Track: The front track is slightly larger than the rear. Both feet have only two hooved toes, and there are no dewclaws. The track is shaped like an inverted heart and is taller than wide. The hooves are pointed at the tips, are bulbous at their bases, and have distinctive, concave outer edges. They may splay apart considerably in soft substrates, making the track wider.

Mountain Goat (Rocky Mountain Goat), *Oreamnos americanus*

Family Bovidae (sheep, goats, bison)

Size/Weight: approx. 3' tall at shoulder; approx. 200 lbs. (males larger than females)

Range: Northern Rocky Mountains, northern Cascades

Habitat: High-altitude cliffs, near or above timberline

Found only in North America, the mountain goat is a sturdy, sure-footed member of the bovid family, and the largest mammal likely to be seen in the alpine zone. It is all white or cream colored, with dense, wooly fur and a shaggy beard below the throat. The hooves and the thin, backward-curving horns are black. Horns are present in both males and females. The shoulder is humped, and the tail is short and stubby. Able to withstand extreme cold, mountain goats are seen singly or in small groups foraging among impossibly steep, rocky slopes for lichens, grasses, herbs, ferns, and tree branches.

Track size (front): 3" wide x 3" long

Track size (rear): 2¾" wide x 2½" long

Description of Track: The front track is larger than the rear. Both feet have four toes, with two hooved inner toes and two outer dewclaws that do not register in the track, but are important to assist in gripping steep terrain. The tips of the hooves are pointed in the center, not to the inside as in other bovids. There is a large subunguinis, which also aids in traction. The hoof points may splay apart considerably.

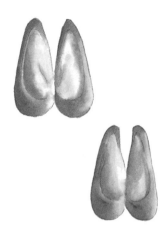

Bighorn Sheep, *Ovis canadensis*

Family Bovidae (sheep, goats, bison)

Size/Weight: approx. 3′ tall at shoulder, body 6′ long; approx. 250 lbs. (males larger than females)

Range: Western United States

Habitat: Rugged, mountainous areas

The bighorn sheep is the largest of the true sheep, and consists of subspecies in the Rocky Mountains, the Sierra Nevada, and the desert Southwest. It is closely related to the Dall's sheep of Alaska and Western Canada. It is stocky and colored light brown to grayish with a white rump and backs of the legs. Both sexes have horns, but those of the male are much larger, curve in an arc to the back, and can weigh up to 25 pounds. They are used in dramatic head-butting rituals during the mating season. Sure-footed and agile, bighorn sheep form groups and forage on all variety of plants and tree branches, and are able to eat very dry and tough material.

Track size (front): 2½″ wide x 3″ long
Track size (rear): 2″ wide x 2¾″ long

Description of Track: The front track is larger than the rear. Both feet have four toes, with two hooved inner toes and two outer dew-claws that do not register in the track. The tips of the hooves are bluntly pointed, with tips slightly to the inside of the track. There is a large subunguinis, which aids in traction on steep slopes.

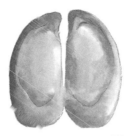

Bison, *Bison bison*

Family Bovidae (sheep, goats, bison)

Size/Weight: approx. 6' tall at shoulder, body 8' long; approx. 1,200 lbs. (males larger than females)

Range: Isolated regions of central and western United States

Habitat: Grassy plains, open woodlands

The largest land mammal in North America, the bison is a massive bovid that once roamed huge expanses of the continent but is now limited to small pockets of protected areas. It has a humped back and large head with curving horns in both sexes. The color is brownish with a thick, shaggy, darker head and forequarters. Bison are fast runners for their size, are active during the day, and are gregarious. They form large grazing herds, eating mostly grasses and sedges, and spend much of their day wallowing or chewing their cud.

Track size (front): 5¾" wide x 5¾" long
Track size (rear): 5½" wide x 5½" long

Description of Track: The front track is larger than the rear, and there is a prominent ridge between the hooves. Both feet have four toes, with two hooved inner toes and two outer dewclaws that do not register in the track. As a whole, the track appears very round, with each hoof forming a semicircle. At the back of the track is a distinctive, angled division where the pad meets the subunguinis. The shape of the track is much like that of domestic cattle, but much larger.

Wild Boar (Feral Pig), *Sus scrofa*

Family Suidae (wild boars)

Size/Weight: body approx. 4′ long, tail approx. 6″ long; approx. 200 lbs. or more
Range: Scattered areas of midwest, southeast, Texas, and California
Habitat: Forests, open woodlands, swamps

Wild boars are either the feral populations of domesticated pigs, the introduced wild boars from Europe, or hybrids of the two. They have a stocky body with short, thin legs and a large head with a protruding snout. The male wild boar has canines that are enlarged into tusks. The hair is bristly and thick and varies in color from black to brownish to white. Fast-moving and quite aggressive, they are active mostly during the morning and evening, and can be found alone or in groups. They forage on the move, digging up roots and tubers, grazing on plants, or hunting insects.

Track size (front): 2½″ wide x 2½″ long
Track size (rear): 2″ wide x 2″ long (without dewclaws)
Description of Track: The front track is larger than the rear. Both feet have four toes, with two hooved inner toes and two prominent, pointed dewclaws that register behind and to the sides. The hooves are pointed at the tips, bulbous at the base, and curved convexly along the outside edges and concavely along the inside edges. The toes may splay apart considerably, giving a wider track.

Collared Peccary (Javelina), *Pecari tajacu*

Family Tayassuidae (Peccaries)

Size/Weight: body approx. 34" long, tail approx. 1" long; approx. 40 lbs.

Range: Southwestern and south-central United States

Habitat: Arid semi-desert, brush, chaparral

The collared peccary is a native, active, piglike mammal of Mexico and Central America whose range just comes up to the United States. It is smaller than the wild boar, and is stocky and big-headed with short, thin legs and a long snout. Its hair is coarse and colored a mix of black and gray, with a pale collar behind the neck. They move in small groups, often traveling along the same paths, using their sensitive snouts to probe for roots, cacti, insects, and nuts. Usually active in morning or late afternoon, except in winter when they may be active all day. They are able to jump quite far and can swim as well.

Track size (front): 1½" wide x 1½" long

Track size (rear): 1¼" wide x 1½" long

Description of Track: Both feet have two inner, hooved toes that are quite blunt at their tips. The front foot has two outer dewclaws that are positioned high off the foot and do not normally register, while the hind foot has only one dewclaw. The surface of the track is fairly flat. The track is similar to that of the wild boar, but smaller, blunter, and with no dewclaw imprint except in deep substrates.

Nine-banded Armadillo, *Dasypodidae novemcinctus*
Family Dasypodidae (Armadillos)
Size/Weight: body approx. 31" long with tail; approx. 12 lbs.
Range: Southeastern United States
Habitat: Woodlands, scrub, arroyos

The nine-banded armadillo is a curious, largely tropical mammal with an armored back made of small plates of hornlike material. It has a pointed head, large ears, short limbs, and a long, scaled tail that is about the same length as the body. It is colored uniform gray. Armadillos are mostly solitary and active during low-light hours. They are excellent diggers, make extensive burrows, and are comfortable in the water. They forage on the ground primarily for insects and worms, but will also eat fruit, eggs, or other invertebrates, lapping up food with their sticky tongues.

Track size (front): 1½" wide x 1¾" long
Track size (rear): 2" wide x 2½" long
Description of Track: There are four toes on the front foot, with the two inner toes being much longer than the two outer toes. There are five toes on the rear foot, with the two outer toes also being shorter and to the sides. All toes register along their entire length, from tip to palm. The claws are long and stout for digging, and are almost always present in the track. Metacarpal pads are partly fused and indistinct from the rest of the palm. Often, only the inner toes of both feet will register.

BIRDS

Canada Goose, *Branta canadensis*
Family Anatidae (Ducks, Geese)
Size: 27–35"
Range: Throughout the United States
Habitat: Marshes, grasslands, public parks, golf courses

The Canada goose is very common and is often found in suburban settings. It is vegetarian, foraging on land for grass, seeds, and grain or in the water by upending like the dabbling ducks. It has a heavy body with short, thick legs and a long neck. Overall it is barred gray-brown with a white rear, short black tail, black neck, and a white patch running under the neck to behind the eye. During its powerful flight in the classic V formation, the white across the rump makes a semicircular patch between the tail and back. Voice is a loud honk.

Track size: 4½" wide x 4½" long
Description of Track: Feet are artiodactyl, with toe one to the rear and toes two, three, and four to the front. The two outer toes curve up, giving the track a semicircular appearance. The rear toe is very small and registers as a small projection at the base of the foot, or simply as a claw imprint. The most obvious feature is the complete webbing of the front toes to aid in swimming. Front claws are short and blunt, either registering with the toes or being slightly separate. The usual gait is a walk, and the track is similar to other geese, varying mainly by size.

Mallard, *Anas platyrhynchos*
Family Anatidae (Ducks, Geese)
Size: 23"
Range: Throughout the United States
Habitat: Virtually any water environment, parks, urban areas

The ubiquitous mallard is the most abundant duck in the northern hemisphere. It is a classic dabbling duck, plunging its head into the water with its tail up, searching for aquatic plants, animals, and snails, although it will also eat worms, seeds, insects, and even mice. Noisy and quacking, it is heavy but is a strong flier. The male has a dark head with green or blue iridescence, a white neck ring, and a large yellow bill. The underparts are pale with a chestnut-brown breast. The female is plain brownish, with buff scalloped markings, and has a dark eye-line and an orangey bill with a dark center. The speculum is blue on both sexes, and the tail coverts often curl upward. Mallards form huge floating flocks called "rafts." To achieve flight, it lifts straight into the air without running.

Track size: 3" wide x 2¾" long
Description of Track: Feet are artiodactyl, with toe one to the rear and toes two, three, and four to the front. The two outer toes curve toward the center, giving the foot a semicircular appearance. The rear toe is very small and registers as a small projection at the base of the foot, or simply as a claw imprint. There is complete webbing of the front toes, which curves in toward the base of the foot more so than with the geese. The claws are short and blunt and usually not separate from the toes in the track. Feet turn inward in its normal waddling, walking gait. The track is similar to most dabbling ducks, differing mostly by size.

Wild Turkey, *Meleagris gallopavo*
Family Phasianidae (Pheasants, Grouse, Turkeys)
Size: 36–48", males larger than females
Range: Throughout the United States
Habitat: Open mixed woodlands

The wild turkey is a very large (though slimmer than the domestic variety), dark, ground-dwelling bird. The legs are thick and stout, and the heavily barred plumage is quite iridescent in strong light. The head and neck appear small for the body size and are covered with bluish, warty, crinkled bare skin that droops under the chin in a red wattle. Often foraging in flocks, they roam the ground for seeds, grubs, and insects and then roost at night in trees. Males emit the familiar *gobble,* while females are less vocal, making a soft clucking sound. In display, the male will hunch with its tail up and spread like a giant fan. Southwestern races show white banding on the tail.

Track size: 4½" wide x 4½" long

Description of Track: Feet are very large and artiodactyl, with toe one to the rear and toes two, three, and four to the front. The front toes are large and of almost equal length, while the rear toe is smaller and raised up so that it may not register, or register only as a claw mark. The other claws are usually visible in the track and close to the toe tips. Its common gait is a walk, and there is a prominent metatarsal pad.

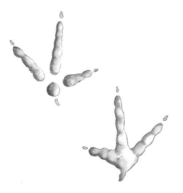

Ring-necked Pheasant, *Phasianus colchicus*
Family Phasianidae (Pheasants, Grouse, Turkeys)
Size: 21–34", females larger than males
Range: Northern and central United States
Habitat: Grasslands, woodland edges, agricultural land with brushy cover

The ring-necked pheasant is a large, beautifully colored, chicken-shaped bird with a very long, pointed tail. The male is ornately patterned rufous, gold, and blue-gray, with pale spotting on the wings and back and dark spotting underneath. The head is dark iridescent green-blue with extensive red facial skin and a tufted crown. There is a clean white ring about the neck. The female is much plainer, mottled brown above and plain below, without obvious head markings. Ring-necked pheasants peck on the ground for seeds, grasses, and insects. Sounds include a harsh, two-syllabled *auk-CAW* vocalization and muffled wing fluttering. They are strong runners and flyers.

Track size: 2¾" wide x 2¾" long
Description of Track: Feet are artiodactyl, with toe one to the rear and toes two, three, and four to the front. The front toes are broad and show some segmentation, while the rear toe is smaller and raised up so that it usually registers only as a claw mark. The other claws are thick, visible in the track, and close to the toe tips. Its common gait is a walk, and there is a prominent metatarsal pad.

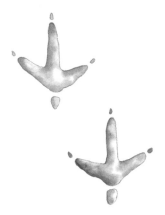

White-tailed Ptarmigan, *Lagopus leucura*
Family Phasianidae (Pheasants, Grouse, Turkeys)
Size: 13", females larger than males
Range: Rocky Mountains, Pacific mountains
Habitat: High elevations in treeless, mountainous areas; tundra zones

The white-tailed ptarmigan is a small, chunky, grouse-like bird with a small head and bill. Breeding male is white below with dark spotting on the breast and sides, and mottled brown above and on the central tail area. Above the eye is a red comb. Nonbreeding adults of both sexes are all white except for black eyes and bills. The breeding female is mottled brown overall but has white wings and corners of the tail. Legs and toes are feathered for arctic conditions. White-tailed ptarmigans forage on the ground for plant buds, insects, and berries.

Track size: 2" wide x 2½" long
Description of Track: Feet are artiodactyl, with toe one to the rear and toes two, three, and four to the front and larger. The toes are thick and blunt and may be obscured by extensive feathering during the winter. The claws are short and stout, and usually present in the track. Metatarsal pads are not evident. Its common gait is a walk, and may also show the impression of feather tips from takeoffs in deep snow.

BIRDS

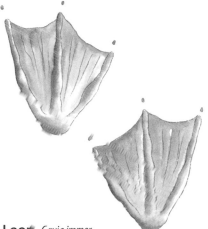

Common Loon, *Gavia immer*
Family Gaviidae (Loons)
Size: 24"
Range: Throughout the United States
Habitat: Coastal waters, inland lakes

Riding low in the water outside the surf zone, this heavy waterbird periodically dives for fish, propelled by its strong webbed feet. Designed for a life in the water, it has legs set far back on its body, which makes walking on land a clumsy affair and takeoff into the air labored. In the winter this bird is usually seen in its drab gray-and-white plumage, unlike the flashy black-and-white spotted plumage it sports during the summer in northern lakes. Its call is a haunting yodel. The common loon can be distinguished from other loons by the horizontal posture of its large bill (not held upward).

Track size: 4¼" wide x 5" long

Description of Track: Feet are artiodactyl, with toe one to the rear and toes two, three, and four to the front and larger. The three forward toes are thin and long, with the fourth toe very small and raised on the leg and not registering in the track. There is complete webbing between the forward toes to aid in swimming. The claws are short but may appear as dots in the track. There is a prominent metatarsal depression. The gait is a clumsy walk, often accompanied by drag from the breast.

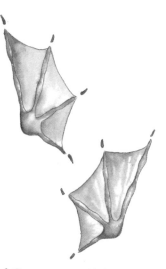

Double-crested Cormorant, *Phalacrocorax auritus*

Family Phalacrocoracidae (Cormorants)

Size: 32"

Range: Throughout the United States

Habitat: Open waters

Named for the two long white plumes that emerge from behind the eyes during breeding season, the double-crested cormorant is an expert swimmer that dives underwater to chase down fish. Because its plumage lacks the normal oils to repel water, it will stand with wings outstretched to dry itself. It is all black, with a pale glossy cast on the back and wings. The eyes are bright green, the bill is thin and hooked, and the throat patch and lores are yellow.

Track size: 4" wide x 4½" long

Description of Track: Feet are artiodactyl, with toe one to the rear and toes two, three, and four to the front, but the configuration is unique whereby the hind toe is rotated to the inside, and the longest toe is the front, outside toe. All toes are very thin and straight. The feet have a condition known as *totipalmate*, where all toes are completely webbed—an adaptation for a highly aquatic lifestyle. The claws are long and thin, and usually register in the track. It is a similar track to pelican, but the toes are not as robust.

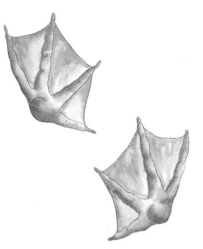

American White Pelican, *Pelecanus erythrorhynchos*
Family Pelecanidae (Pelicans)
Size: 62"
Range: Most of the United States except the northeast
Habitat: Open freshwater

One of North America's largest birds, the American white pelican has a wingspan of over 9 feet. It is white overall, with black flight feathers. The massive bill is orange and has a membranous, expandable throat pouch. In posture, it holds its neck in a characteristic strong kink and its folded wings in a peak along its back. American white pelicans often feed in cooperative groups, herding fish as they swim and scooping them up by dipping their bills in the water. They never plunge-dive like the brown pelican. When breeding, a strange horny growth appears on the upper mandible in both sexes.

Track size: 4¾" wide x 5½" long

Description of Track: Feet are artiodactyl, with toe one to the rear and toes two, three, and four to the front, but like the cormorants, the hind toe is rotated to the inside. All toes are fairly robust and straight. The feet have a condition known as *totipalmate,* where all toes are completely webbed—an adaptation for a highly aquatic lifestyle. The claws are short and broad, and usually register in the track in connection with the toes. The gait is a walk, and the track is similar to the brown pelican.

Great Blue Heron, *Ardea herodias*
Family Ardeidae (Herons, Egrets)
Size: 46″
Range: Throughout the United States
Habitat: Most aquatic areas, including lakes, creeks, and marshes

The great blue heron is the largest heron in North America. Walking slowly through shallow water or fields, it stalks fish, crabs, and small vertebrates, catching them with its massive bill. With long legs and a long neck, it is blue-gray overall, with a white face and a heavy yellow-orange bill. The crown is black and supports plumes of medium length. The front of the neck is white, with distinct black chevrons fading into breast plumes. In flight, the neck is tucked back and the wingbeats are regular and labored.

Track size: 5″ wide x 6 ¾″ long

Description of Track: Feet are artiodactyl, with toe one to the rear and toes two, three, and four to the front. All toes are long and narrow, with the hind toe nearly as long as the front ones. The hind toe is slightly offset to the inside, not meeting at the exact center of the foot. There is a small amount of webbing near the base of the toes, and the metatarsal pad is often not evident. The claws are short but usually register. The normal gait is a walk, and the track is similar to other herons, differing mainly by size.

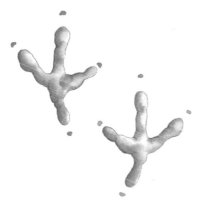

Red-tailed Hawk, *Buteo jamaicensis*

Family Accipitridae (Hawks, Eagles)
Size: 20"
Range: Throughout the United States
Habitat: Open country, prairies

This widespread species is the most common buteo in the United States. It has broad, rounded wings and a stout, hooked bill. Its plumage is highly variable depending on geographic location. In general, the underparts are light with darker streaking that forms a dark band across the belly, the upperparts are dark brown, and the tail is rufous. Light spotting occurs along the scapulars. In flight, there is a noticeable dark patch along the inner leading edge of the underwing. Red-tailed hawks glide down from perches, such as telephone poles and posts in open country, to catch rodents, and they may also hover to spot prey. They are usually seen alone or in pairs. Voice is the familiar *keeer!*

Track size: 3" wide x 4" long
Description of Track: Feet are artiodactyl, with toe one to the rear and toes two, three, and four to the front. All toes are thick with bulbous segments and blunt tips. The rear toe is nearly as long as the front ones. The claws are long and curved for gripping prey, as in most raptors, and are usually obvious in the track. The central metatarsal pad is not prominent. The track is similar to other hawks, varying mostly by size.

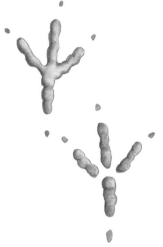

Bald Eagle, *Haliaeetus leucocephalus*
Family Accipitridae (Hawks, Eagles)
Size: 30–40", females larger than males
Range: Throughout the United States
Habitat: Lakes, rivers with tall perches or cliffs

The bald eagle is a large raptor that is widespread but fairly uncommon. It eats fish or scavenges dead animals, and congregates in large numbers where food is abundant. Its plumage is dark brown, contrasting with its white head and tail. Juveniles show white splotching across the wings and breast. The yellow bill is large and powerful, and the talons are large and sharp. In flight, it holds its wings fairly flat and straight, resembling a long plank. Bald eagles make huge nests of sticks high in trees.

Track size: 4" wide x 6 ½" long

Description of Track: Feet are artiodactyl, with toe one to the rear and toes two, three, and four to the front. All toes are thick with bulbous segments and blunt tips. The rear toe is nearly as long as the front ones. The claws are long and curved for gripping prey, as in most raptors, and register some distance from the end of the toes. The central metatarsal pad is not prominent, and often there is a negative space in the center of the track. The normal gait is a walk, and the track is similar to the golden eagle.

72

American Coot, *Fulica americana*
Family Rallidae (Rails, Coots)
Size: 15"
Range: Throughout the United States
Habitat: Wetlands, ponds, urban lawns and parks

The American coot has a plump body and a thick head and neck. It is a very common bird and becomes relatively tame in urban areas and parks. It dives for fish to feed, but it will also dabble like a duck or pick food from the ground. It is dark gray overall, with a black head and white bill that ends with a dark narrow ring. The white trailing edge of the wings can be seen in flight. The toes are flanked with lobes that enable the coot to walk on water plants and swim efficiently. Juveniles are similar in plumage to adults but paler. Coots are often seen in very large flocks.

Track size: 2" wide x 2½" long
Description of Track: Feet are artiodactyl, with toe one to the rear and toes two, three, and four to the front. The hind toe is very short, and the front toes are long, narrow, and flanked by wide, indented lobes that spread as the foot passes back through the water for propulsion. The claws are usually evident in the track, and there is a prominent metatarsal pad. The normal gait is a walk, and the track is similar to grebes, except that the lobing on grebes is not indented.

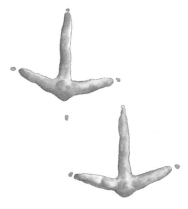

Sandhill Crane, *Grus canadensis*
Family Gruidae (Cranes)
Size: 45"
Range: Throughout the United States
Habitat: Fields, shallow wetlands

The sandhill crane is a tall bird with long, strong legs, a long neck, and a long, straight bill. The long, thick, tertial feathers create the distinctive bustle on the rear of all cranes. The top of the head is covered by bare red skin. Plumage is gray overall but may become spotted with rust-colored stains caused by preening with a bill stained by iron-rich mud. In flocks, it grazes in fields, gleaning grains, insects, and small animals, and returns to protected wetland areas in the evening to roost. The voice of the sandhill crane is a throaty, penetrating trumpeting sound. Unlike herons, it flies in groups with its neck extended.

Track size: 5" wide x 4½" long

Description of Track: Feet are artiodactyl, with toe one to the rear and toes two, three, and four to the front. The front toes are robust and long, with the outer ones often spreading wide to the sides in an almost inverted T shape to support this huge bird. The rear toes are very small and raised on the foot, so usually they do not register in the track except for the claws. Other claws are short and blunt and may or may not register. The metatarsal pad is large and prominent. The common gait is a walk, and the track is similar to that of the whooping crane, which is slightly larger.

Killdeer, *Charadrius vociferus*
Family Charadriidae (Plovers)
Size: 10"
Range: Throughout the United States
Habitat: Inland fields, farmlands, lakeshores, meadows

The killdeer gets its name from its piercing *kill-dee* call, which is often heard before these well-camouflaged plovers are seen. Well adapted to human-altered environments, it is quite widespread and gregarious. It has long, pointed wings, a long tail, and a conspicuous double-banded breast. The upper parts are dark brown, the belly is white, and the head is patterned with a white supercilium and forehead. The tail is rusty orange with a black tip. In flight, there is a noticeable white stripe across the flight feathers. The killdeer is known for the classic "broken wing" display that it uses to distract predators from its nest and young.

Track size: 1¼" wide x 1¾" long

Description of Track: Feet are artiodactyl, with toe one to the rear and toes two, three, and four to the front. The toes are narrow, with the outer ones aligned far to the sides next to the long, straight, central toe. The rear toe is short and often not pronounced in the track. The claws are short and usually register as pointed extensions of the toes. This track pattern is common for most shorebirds, although sizes vary, and some exhibit minor webbing between the toes. The normal gait is a walk or run.

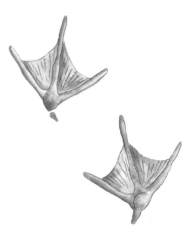

American Avocet, *Recurvirostra americana*

Family Recurvirostridae (Avocets, Stilts)
Size: 18"
Range: Western United States and eastern coastal regions
Habitat: Shallow wetlands, marshes

The elegant American avocet has a long, delicate, upturned black bill and long, thin, blue-gray legs. The upperparts are patterned black and white, the belly is white, and the head and neck are light orange-brown punctuated by black eyes. The bill of the female is slightly shorter than that of the male and has a greater bend. Nonbreeding adults have a pale gray head and neck. Avocets use a side-to-side sweeping motion of the bill to stir up small crustaceans and insect larvae as they wade methodically through the shallows. They may even submerge their heads as the water deepens. They are adept swimmers and emit a *wheet!* call in alarm.

Track size: 2¾" wide x 2½" long

Description of Track: Feet are artiodactyl, with toe one to the rear and toes two, three, and four to the front. The front toes are slender, and the rear toe is very small and often does not register in the track. Being food swimmers, avocets have webbing between the front toes that comes to about halfway up the foot. The claws are small and not obvious in the track, and there is a prominent metatarsal pad. The normal gait is a walk.

Herring Gull, *Larus argentatus*
Family Laridae (Gulls, Terns)
Size: 25"
Range: Throughout the United States
Habitat: Wetlands, coastal beaches, fields

The widespread herring gull occurs across the North American continent. It is a large, relatively thin, white-headed gull with a pale gray back and white underparts. The bill is thick and yellow, with a reddish spot at the tip of the lower mandible. The primaries are black with white-spotted tips. The nonbreeding adult has brown streaking across the nape and neck. The legs are pink, and the eyes are pale yellow to ivory colored. Herring gulls are opportunistic feeders, eating fish, worms, crumbs, and trash. They are known to drop shellfish from the air to crack open their shells.

Track size: 3" wide x 2¾" long

Description of Track: Feet are artiodactyl, with toe one to the rear and toes two, three, and four to the front. The three forward toes are of almost equal length, and the outer toes are fairly straight, unlike the inward-curving toes of the ducks and geese. The rear toe is very small and often does not register, or does so only as a small dot of the claw. The complete webbing between the front toes is relatively straight across but may not register clearly on hard surfaces. This track is similar to other gulls, differing mostly by size.

Barred Owl, *Strix varia*
Family Strigidae (Typical Owls)
Size: 21"
Range: Eastern and northwestern United States
Habitat: Wooded swamps, upland forests

The barred owl is a large, compact owl with a short tail and wings, rounded head, and big, dark eyes. It lacks the ear tufts seen on the great horned owl, and has comparatively small talons. Plumage is gray-brown overall with dark barring on the neck and breast, turning to streaking on the belly and flanks. It swoops from its perch to catch small rodents, frogs, or snakes. Its voice, often heard during the day, is a hooting, "who-cooks-for-you," or a kind of bark. Nest is made in tree cavities vacated by other species.

Track size: 2" wide x 3" long

Description of Track: Feet are zygodactyl, whereby two toes point forward, one points to the back, and one can either be placed to the side or to the back, forming an "X" or "K" shape. The toes are thick and blunt, as in most raptorial species, and the claws are thick and prominent. Most owls show this foot arrangement.

Northern Flicker, *Colaptes auratus*
Family Picidae (Woodpeckers)
Size: 12½"
Range: Throughout the United States
Habitat: Variety of habitats, including suburbs and parks

The common northern flicker is a large, long-tailed woodpecker often seen foraging on the ground for ants and other small insects. It is barred brown and black across the back, and buff with black spotting below. The head is brown, with a gray nape and crown. On the upper breast is a prominent half-circle of black, and the male has a red patch at the malar region. Flight is undulating and shows an orange wing lining and white rump. Its voice is a loud, sharp *keee*, and it will sometimes drum its bill repeatedly at objects, like a jackhammer. The northern flicker is sometimes referred to as the red-shafted flicker.

Track size: ½" wide x 2" long
Description of Track: Feet are zygodactyl, whereby two toes point forward and two toes point backward, giving extra support while perched on vertical tree trunks. Compared to the usual toe arrangement, the outside back toe has rotated to the rear. All toes are long and thin, and create a narrow X-shaped pattern. The claws are long and curved, and usually register. The gait is a walk, and the track is similar to most woodpeckers, differing mainly by size.

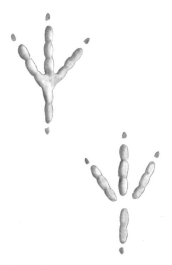

Black-billed Magpie, *Pica hudsonia*

Family Corvidae (Jays, Crows)
Size: 19"
Range: Western United States
Habitat: Riparian areas, open woodlands, pastures, rural areas

The black-billed magpie is a heavy, broad-winged bird with an extremely long, graduated tail. It has striking pied plumage, being black on the head, upper breast, and back, dark iridescent green-blue on the wings and tail, and crisp white on the scapulars and belly. The legs are dark and stout, and the bill is thick at the base. Juvenile birds have a much shorter tail. Magpies travel in small groups, and are opportunistic feeders of insects, nuts, eggs, or carrion. The voice is a whining, questioning *mag?* or a harsh *wok-wok.*

Track size: 1½" wide x 2¼" long

Description of Track: Feet are artiodactyl, with toe one to the rear and toes two, three, and four to the front. All toes are thick with well-defined digital pads, and all are almost equal in length. The track lacks a metatarsal pad, which often leaves an open area in the center. The claws are fairly long and thick, and usually obvious in the track. Magpies use a walking or hopping gait, and their tracks are similar to the raven and crow but smaller and less robust.

Common Raven   *Corvus corax*
Family Corvidae (Jays, Crows)
Size: 24"
Range: Western United States, eastern mountains
Habitat: Occupies a wide range of habitats including deserts, mountains, canyons, and forests

The common raven is a stocky, gruff, large corvid with a long, massive bill that slopes directly into the forehead. The wings are narrow and long, and the tail is rounded or wedge-shaped. The entire body is glossy black, sometimes bluish, and the neck is laced with pointed, shaggy feathers. Quite omnivorous, it feeds on carrion, refuse, insects, and roadkill, and has a varied voice that includes deep croaking. Ravens may soar and engage in rather acrobatic flight. Crows are similar but are smaller, with proportionately smaller bills.

Track size: 1¾" wide x 3½" long
Description of Track: Feet are artiodactyl, with toe one in the rear and toes two, three, and four to the front. All toes are robust with prominent pads and thinner, interdigital pads as well as the front toes. The rear toe is as long as the two outer toes. There is no prominent metatarsal pad, and the foot often leaves no imprint at the heel area. The claws are long, thick, curved, and usually register. The gait is a walk or hop, and similar to the crow but larger.

American Robin, *Turdus migratorius*
Family Turdidae (Thrushes)
Size: 10″
Range: Throughout the United States
Habitat: Widespread in a variety of habitats, including woodlands, fields, parks, lawns

Familiar and friendly, the American robin is a large thrush with long legs and a long tail. It commonly holds its head cocked and keeps its wing tips lowered beneath its tail. It is gray brown above and rufous below, with a darker head and contrasting white eye crescents and loral patches. The chin is streaked black and white and the bill is yellow with darker edges. Females are typically paler overall, and the juvenile shows spots of white above and dark spots below. Robins forage on the ground, picking out earthworms and insects, or in trees for berries. The robin's song is a series of high, musical phrases, sounding like *cheery, cheer-u-up, cheerio*.

Track size: 1¼″ wide x 2″ long

Description of Track: Feet are artiodactyl, with toe one to the rear and toes two, three, and four to the front. The rear toe is nearly as long as the front three. All toes are thin, and sometimes thicker toward the tips. The claws are medium length and often appear separate from the toes. The metatarsal pad is not evident, often resulting in a bare space in the center of the track. The gait is a hop or a walk. This is a typical songbird track pattern, with considerable variability in size and amount of splay between the toes.

REPTILES

Eastern Fence Lizard, *Sceloporus undulatus*

Family Iguanidae (Fence Lizards)
Size: 6″ long with tail
Range: Southern parts of the United States except California
Habitat: Grasslands, woodlands; brushy, sunny areas

The eastern fence lizard includes several subspecies of varying color patterns including grayish or brownish, with either longitudinal striping, spotting, or a combination thereof. It is a compact, long-tailed lizard with big feet, a blunt face, and scaled, dry skin. Solitary and active during the day, fence lizards scurry through sheltered areas or among trees for all kinds of insects and other invertebrates.

Track size (front): ¼″ wide x ¾″ long
Track size (rear): ¼″ wide x 1″ long
Description of Track: There are five toes on both the front and rear feet. The toes are long and thin (especially the outer, forward toe of the rear foot) and attached to a broad palm. The claws are small and pointed, and may or may not register in the track. The tracks tend to point outward in a walk, and may be accompanied by tail or body drag. This species is closely related to the western fence lizard of the Pacific states.

Snapping Turtle, *Chelydra serpentina*

Family Chelydridae (Snapping Turtles)

Size: 14" long (males larger than females)

Range: Central and eastern United States

Habitat: Most freshwater aquatic environments, especially with plentiful water plants

The snapping turtle is a large, stocky turtle with a relatively small shell for its body size, a long, tapered tail, and a massive head with powerful jaws. Its color is variable shades of brown but is often obscured by a coating of algae. The feet are strong with long claws. Snapping turtles may rest underwater on muddy bottoms, or bask on rocks in the sun, and they hibernate during the cold season. They forage for a wide variety of food, including plants, insects, aquatic invertebrates, or even small mammals and birds.

Track size (front): 2" wide x 1½" long

Track size (rear): 2¼" wide x 3" long

Description of Track: There are five toes on the front foot and four on the rear. The foot is an oblong, relatively flat pad with few distinguishing marks or ridges. The claws are fairly long and stout, and usually register in the track as dots. The front foot tends to point inward, the rear foot straight ahead, and tail drag may be apparent.

American Alligator, *Alligator mississippiensis*
Family Alligatoridae (Alligators)
Size: approx. 12' long (males larger than females)
Range: Southeast Gulf states
Habitat: Most aquatic environments, fresh or brackish swamps

The American alligator is a reptile of the south and is the largest in North America. Once threatened with extinction, it is now protected and is maintaining stable populations. It is strong and compact with short limbs and a long, thick head with a rounded snout and imposing, teeth-laden jaws. Its skin is lined with ridges along the back, and colored gray to greenish, paler underneath. Adept swimmers, alligators move slowly on land except for occasional, rapid lunges. They are omnivorous and will eat almost any available food, including fish, other reptiles, birds, or mammals to the size of livestock.

Track size (front): 8" wide x 10" long
Track size (rear): 10" wide x 12" long
Description of Track: There are five toes on the front foot and four on the rear. The outer toe of the front foot is far to the rear and outside, and all toes are thick and stubby. The rear foot shows a long heel with a pebbled texture, and has partial webbing between the central toes. The large, strong claws are usually evident in the track. The normal gait is a walk, and the tracks may be obscured by tail or body drag. The track is similar to the American crocodile, which has a range restricted to southern Florida.

REPTILES

Snakes, (many species)
Suborder Serpentes (snakes)
Size: variable
Range: Throughout the United States
Habitat: Most habitats, depending on species

Snakes are long, round, slender, scaled reptiles with no limbs. Propulsion is provided by contraction and expansion of the highly muscled and flexible body. They are nocturnal or diurnal, and inhabit a wide variety of locations from mountains to deserts to streams. Requiring warm temperature to be active, snakes hibernate or become dormant in cold weather. All are carnivorous, and use their flexible jaws to swallow prey whole.

Track size: varies
Description of Track: There is no footprint, of course, but markings left by the underside of the body. This trail is represented by a series of parallel ridges or grooves in the substrate that emulate a loose S shape—either very stretched out or compacted. Snakes known as sidewinders move sideways to the direction of travel, gaining traction on one section of the body and lifting the rest to a new forward position.

AMPHIBIANS

American Toad, *Bufo americanus*

Family Bufonidae (Toads)
Size: approx. 3¼" long
Range: Eastern United States except the far South
Habitat: Areas near fresh water; woodlands, fields, urban lawns

Adapted to moist environments, the American toad is a squat, plump amphibian with stocky limbs, strong rear legs, and a short face. It has lumpy skin with enlarged warts and is colored variable shades of brown or green with darker spotting and a pale stripe down the back. There is a distinctive pair of bean-shaped paratoid glands behind the eyes that secrete a foul-tasting, milky substance to deter predators. Toads are mostly nocturnal, and they hop or walk among vegetation, rocks and logs foraging for all variety of insects, worms, and larvae. During the winter they nestle into a burrow to hibernate.

Track size (front): ½" wide x ¾" long
Track size (rear): 1" wide x 1¼" long
Description of Track: The front track is smaller than the rear and is angled inward toward the body. There are four toes on the front foot and five on the rear, and there is partial webbing between all toes on the rear. Claws are absent. The heel impression of front and rear feet shows small, bulbous protrusions. The tracks may be obscured by dragging of the feet. The track is similar to other toads but has less webbing than the frogs.

Northern Leopard Frog, *Rana pipiens*
Family Ranidae (True Frogs)
Size: approx. 4" long
Range: Across northern United States except the west coast
Habitat: Freshwater or brackish marshes; streams, ponds

The northern leopard frog is a squat, boney amphibian with narrow hindquarters and long, powerful rear legs for leaping. There are two, pale, narrow ridges of skin along either side of the back, and there is a light stripe above the mouth. The overall color of its smooth skin is green to brownish with large, dark spots bordered by a lighter color, giving the frog its common name. Leopard frogs skulk in the water or vegetation foraging for insects and invertebrates. Their large mouths allow them to eat fairly large prey, including small birds or other frogs.

Track size (front): ½" wide x ¾" long
Track size (rear): 1" wide x 1¼" long
Description of Track: The front track is smaller than the rear, and is angled inward toward the body. There are four toes on the front foot and five long, thin toes on the rear, with webbing present on the rear foot only. Claws are absent. The heel impression of front and rear feet is smooth, with no bulbous protrusions as in some toads. The gait is a walk, hop, or erratic leaping pattern. The track is similar to that of the southern leopard frog of southeastern United States.

Bullfrog, *Rana catesbeiana*

Family Ranidae (True Frogs)
Size: approx. 6" long
Range: Eastern United States, isolated areas in the West and Pacific states
Habitat: Ponds, lakes; prefers dense vegetation

Our largest frog, the bullfrog is squat and heavy-bodied with massive rear legs allowing quick, strong leaps and swimming. Its smooth skin is green to brownish-green with brown or gray mottling or spotting, and a pale belly. It has large, external eardrums just behind the eyes. Bullfrogs are mostly nocturnal and always found in or near a body of water. Their large mouths enable them to feed on a wide variety of prey, including insects, aquatic invertebrates, and even small mammals or birds.

Track size (front): 1" wide x 1½" long
Track size (rear): 1" wide x 2" long
Description of Track: The front track is smaller than the rear, and is angled inward toward the body. There are four toes on the front foot and five long, thin toes on the rear. There is complete webbing between all toes on the rear, except for between the two outer toes, where the webbing only comes part way up the longer toe. Claws are absent. The heel impression of front and rear feet is smooth, with no bulbous protrusions as in some toads. The gait is a walk or hop, sometimes with considerable drag from the large belly. The track is similar to that of other frogs but much larger.

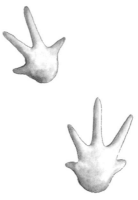

Eastern Newt, *Notophthalmus viridescens*
Family Salamandridae (Newts)
Size: approx. 4" long
Range: Eastern United States
Habitat: Wetlands, ponds, and accompanying meadows and woodlands

Newts are elongate, short-legged, long-tailed, semi-aquatic relatives of the salamanders with rough-textured (not slimy) skin. They are born in the water, mature on land, then return to the water at adulthood. The eastern newt has a coloration that varies from orange in the immature stage to green or brownish in the adult, both with dark spotting overall. Newts are adept swimmers, propelled by undulating their bodies and their long, flattened tails. They forage day or night in the water or on the ground for insects, larvae, fish or frog eggs, and worms. They may burrow during winter months or remain active in areas where water remains unfrozen.

Track size (front): ¼" wide x ¼" long
Track size (rear): ¼" wide x ⅓" long
Description of Track: The front track is about the same size as the rear, and is angled inward toward the body. There are four toes on the front foot and five toes on the rear. The inner toes are long and thin, while the outer toes are much shorter and point to the sides. Claws and webbing are absent. The gait is a slow walk, with limbs remaining far to the outside of the body's center. The track is similar to other species of newts and salamanders.

Index

About the Author/Illustrator

Todd Telander is a naturalist/illustrator/artist living in Walla Walla, Washington. He has studied and illustrated wildlife since 1989, while living in California, Colorado, New Mexico, and Washington.

He graduated from the University of California at Santa Cruz with degrees in biology, environmental studies, and scientific illustration and has since illustrated numerous books and other publications, including other Falcon Field Guides and FalconGuides' Scats and Tracks series. His wife, Kirsten Telander, is a writer, and he has two sons, Miles and Oliver. His work can be viewed online at www.toddtelander.com.